D1601395

Finding One's Place: Teaching Styles and
Peer Relations in Diverse Classrooms
STEPHEN PLANK

PreMed: Who Makes It and Why
MARY ANN MAGUIRE

Tracking Inequality: Stratification and Mobility in
American High Schools
SAMUEL ROUNDFIELD LUCAS

Working for Equity in Heterogeneous Classrooms:
Sociological Theory in Practice
Edited by ELIZABETH G. COHEN and RACHEL A. LOTAN

Who Chooses? Who Loses?: Culture, Institutions, and the
Unequal Effects of School Choice
Edited by BRUCE FULLER and RICHARD F. ELMORE
with GARY ORFIELD

Hosting Newcomers: Structuring Educational Opportunities
for Immigrant Children
ROBERT A. DENTLER and ANNE L. HAFNER

Mandating Academic Excellence: High School Responses
to State Curriculum Reform
BRUCE WILSON and GRETCHEN ROSSMAN

From the Series Editor

This volume is based on Stephen Plank's doctoral dissertation, which was awarded the Ron G. Galbraith prize for the sociology of education dissertation of highest quality that had the potential to reach a broad audience as a publishable book. The prize was established in memory of Ron Galbraith, who at the time of his death was a graduate student in sociology of education at Teachers College and an acquisitions editor at Teachers College Press.

Finding One's Place is an important addition not only to the Sociology of Education Series, but also to the larger body of work in sociology of education. This book adds considerably to the small body of research that applies general sociological theory to guide the systematic examination of U.S. classrooms. The decision to utilize general theory results in a more robust and satisfying explanation of the patterns observed in the ten classrooms under study.

There are several distinguishing features of this work. First, it takes advantage of a naturally occurring situation to examine integration in the wake of a desegregation effort. Although the study is framed by this policy of socioeconomic desegregation, it is not constrained by it, as Plank allows the analysis to shift based on his early observations. Second, the study draws on multiple kinds of data to assemble a coherent explanation for patterns of student interaction. All of the data are systematically considered and the multiple parallel analyses reinforce each other. Third, Plank gives serious and sustained consideration to the role of teachers in shaping classroom conditions. Teachers clearly play a major part in determining the nature of the settings in which students are assembled for instruction, and Plank focuses on the ten teachers in the study to reveal their distinctive approaches to organizing their classrooms. These features make the book valuable both for the treatment of the study at hand and for the direction it can lend to further research in the area.

—*Gary Natriello*

FINDING
ONE'S
PLACE

Teaching Styles and Peer Relations in Diverse Classrooms

STEPHEN PLANK
Recipient of the Ron G. Galbraith Sociology of Education Dissertation Prize

Foreword by Sanford M. Dornbusch

Teachers College, Columbia University
New York and London

Published by Teachers College Press, 1234 Amsterdam Avenue, New York, NY 10027

Library of Congress Cataloging-in-Publication Data

Plank, Stephen B.
    Finding one's place : teaching styles and peer relations in diverse
classrooms / Stephen B. Plank ; foreword by Sanford Dornbusch.
       p. cm. — (Sociology of education series)
    Includes bibliographical references (p.   ) and index.
    ISBN 0-8077-3990-1 (cloth : alk. paper) — ISBN 0-8077-3989-8 (pbk. :
alk. paper)
    1. Educational equalization—Wisconsin—LaCrosse—Case studies.
2. Minorities—Education (Elementary)—Wisconsin—LaCrosse—Case
studies. 3. Elementary school teaching—Wisconsin—LaCrosse—Case
studies. 4. Classroom environment—Wisconsin—LaCrosse—Case
studies.   I. Title. II. Sociology of education series (New York, N.Y.)
LC213.23.L33 P53 2000
372.1102—dc21   00-041776

ISBN 0-8077-3989-8 (paper)
ISBN 0-8077-3990-9 (cloth)

Printed on acid-free paper

Manufactured in the United States of America

07   06   05   04   03   02   01   00   8   7   6   5   4   3   2   1

Contents

Foreword

A strength of this book is that it is hard to categorize. Stephen Plank does qualitative studies of the nature of classroom interactions, yet he quantifies his qualitative observations. Case studies of individual students are used to illustrate his perspective, but each individual is always viewed in an ecological context. He portrays the classroom styles of teachers as major determinants of the atmosphere for learning, but he notes that students react in divergent ways to their teachers' attempts to organize the environment. He studies both academic interactions within the classroom and the choice of playmates outside the classroom.

This protean approach pays off. The diversity of topics and methods always has a single goal: to determine how classroom processes can lead to integration among students who differ in gender, social class, and ethnicity. Every analysis is structured to provide greater understanding of the conditions that lead to integration across social boundaries.

Plank's study followed an initiative for the socioeconomic desegregation of the schools of LaCrosse, Wisconsin, that was partly motivated by a desire to reduce the segregation of impoverished Hmong students from Laos, the largest minority in that city. Examining the Hmong experience deserves applause. Plank applies to a small ethnic group general theories of equal status contact that have been developed primarily from studies of larger ethnic and racial minorities. General theories should be applicable to all ethnic groups.

Plank distinguishes between desegregation, which brings previously segregated groups into direct contact, and integration, the subject of this book. Integration is more than contact between members of diverse groups. Integration in classrooms occurs only when students of different backgrounds interact as status equals.

Most studies of desegregation stress the composition of schools and classrooms, but Plank moves beyond this emphasis. Although, as he notes, larger social structures affect the individual class and student, Plank studied the detailed interactions among teachers and students within ten fourth-grade classes drawn from five different LaCrosse schools.

Three times during a school year Plank spent two or three days in each classroom observing the interaction among teachers and students. He collected sociometric data in the fall and spring from each student and interviewed each teacher. Plank ascribes considerable importance to each teacher's development of a task and reward structure, forming a unique social system in each classroom.

Plank categorized each teacher's class in terms of the inclusion of personal references from the lives of the teacher and students, the range of performance settings within the classroom, and the use of less uniform academic and disciplinary standards. These task and reward structures were shown, in both qualitative and quantitative analyses, to affect the structure of peer networks. Along with the students' enrollment histories before and after desegregation, the task and reward structures shaped the interactions among students, the way students learned, and the degree to which the classroom could truly be viewed as integrated.

The findings in this study of ten fourth-grade classrooms are clear and provocative. Future researchers will want to explore related issues with larger samples, longer-term longitudinal studies, and different ethnic groups in more heterogeneous communities. It will also be instructive to examine different age groups in order to observe the impact of developmental processes, such as puberty. For older students, it will be possible to ask several forms of sociometric questions and thereby pinpoint additional aspects of student interaction.

To me, one of the unexpected pleasures of Plank's report is his sensitive portrayal of the teachers' role. His presentation of the differing choices for classroom organization made by each teacher does more than recount what occurs behind closed doors. Plank shows how difficult and intertwined are the decisions that teachers have to make about ways of dealing with their students' academic and nonacademic behavior. Negative consequences can result from decisions that appear perfectly reasonable.

The reader emerges with increased respect for the under-rewarded teachers who must create the social framework for the students in their classrooms. Educators need to devote increased attention to the effects of teacher style and classroom organization upon the social world of students. True integration in schools, a major goal of the larger American society, can occur only if more teachers learn how to make appropriate decisions with respect to the social organization of their classrooms.

Sanford M. Dornbusch,
Stanford, California

Acknowledgments

The inspiration and excitement I felt while completing this book happened, to a great extent, because various people kept letting me know that they thought the work was interesting and important. I want to thank those people.

My appreciation goes first to the administrators, teachers, students, and parents in LaCrosse, Wisconsin. The educators in that school district knew they were trying something unprecedented, controversial, and important as they initiated a socioeconomic balance plan. They were very supportive as they let me into their schools and classrooms to help describe social relations in the wake of the desegregation. I hope my results are useful to that community and others as they make decisions about the organization of their schools. To maintain confidentiality, names of people and schools have been changed throughout the book. Only the name of the city is presented unchanged.

This project began as a doctoral thesis and I greatly appreciate the members of my dissertation committee at the University of Chicago. Charles Bidwell, the chairperson, is an ideal mentor. He offered new ideas and sturdy pushes when I needed them; and he let me struggle and search when I needed that. Charles sees the big picture in a research project and teaches that to his students. James Coleman was on the committee until his death in 1995. He helped me plan and begin this study, and we discussed some of the early analyses. His creativity, energy, and passion remain a huge inspiration to many, including me. Barbara Schneider is another special mentor. I would not have entered graduate school and this profession without her encouraging words to the wide-eyed undergraduate I was during a summer internship in 1989. From that summer forward, Barbara has been teaching me through example how to build teams, teach people, conduct research, and communicate messages. Finally, Gerald Suttles played a special role. Discussing my ideas and findings with him meant moving beyond a tight-knit group of education researchers. His reactions represented to me a test of whether I was revealing stories and processes of general interest and value. Gerry offered creative suggestions, a few needed cautions, and a lot of encouragement.

Since 1995 I have been working at the Center for Social Organization of Schools at Johns Hopkins University. I thank my colleagues at CSOS for their support and encouragement as I turned this project into a book. They are a wonderful group of people working hard to improve education. Sally Adee at CSOS greatly improved the sociograms in Chapter 6.

From Teachers College Press, Susan Liddicoat, Gary Natriello, and an anonymous reviewer were skillful and attentive in guiding me through the process of writing my first book. They did not let me off the hook when difficult improvements needed to be made, but they did let me know that this work was of value and should be finished with good style and substance.

Finally, I thank my family and friends. My parents, Susan and William Plank, have always offered love and encouragement. My wife, Holly, came into my life while I was writing this book. She and I love to help each other keep our hearts and minds healthy. Holly, Mom, Dad, my siblings, and other friends have listened to me babble, worry, exclaim, and complain. Then they've told me jokes. Thanks.

1

Socioeconomic Desegregation and Community Politics

On a Wednesday morning in August 1992, about 4,000 elementary school students began a new year of learning in the public schools of LaCrosse, Wisconsin. Approximately 2,000 of those students stepped aboard yellow school buses that morning. So far nothing was out of the ordinary. This annual ritual is repeated in towns and cities across America every year.

Why, then, had the approach of this school year and these yellow buses held the newspaper headlines in LaCrosse, Milwaukee, and many other cities? Why did the *NBC Nightly News* have cameras and a reporter in LaCrosse on that Wednesday morning? The answer was that 800 of these students were not riding to the same schools they would have attended a year before. Instead, they were crossing the city in one direction or another as a part of a new socioeconomic balance plan.

It was not just these 800 children who were affected by the balance plan. Indeed, they would be the "new kids" in one school or another because of the plan. But virtually all other students in the district's elementary schools would also be affected as they encountered new classmates in their schools. How well would all of these students mix?

Teachers were also affected as they prepared for the school year. Some would have as many as half of their students entering their classrooms because of the balance plan. Others would greet just one or two students who were moving without large contingents of their former classmates. Still others had been assigned to one of the district's newly opening schools where everyone—students, teachers, principal, custodian—would be on new turf. In all these cases, teachers had to decide whether special efforts and changes to their daily routines would be needed to bring their students together to cooperate and learn. If something special or new were needed, what would it be?

Parents were affected as they wondered about the plan's impact on their children's learning. Some had vehemently protested the changes. Some continued to protest. Some had taken advantage of a last-minute opportunity to request transfers for their children back to their former schools. Still others had lauded the balance plan as a wonderful opportunity for community integration and children's growth.

District administrators and school board members were certainly affected. They had weathered months of trying to justify and fine-tune their new school boundaries and busing routes. They had faced community members who had challenged their motives, judgment, and character. Now, finally, on August 26, the buses were rolling, and the new school year would begin.

This book is about the events and social relations in 10 classrooms affected by LaCrosse's socioeconomic balance plan. More generally, though, the book deals with issues that arise any time a group of students and a teacher come together in a combination and setting that did not exist previously. The 10 classrooms in five schools offer insights about the effects on the structure and quality of friendships and peer relations that are caused by the tasks and rewards featured in a classroom and the circumstances that bring a group of children together as classmates. Further, once emerging and evolving peer relations are understood, much can be discovered about students' feelings of belonging and comfort with participation in the daily life of the classroom.

To give context to my investigations into the socioeconomic balance plan implemented by the LaCrosse school district in 1992, I will begin with an overview of the city's geographic setting, economic enterprises, and demographic characteristics including a special look at the city's Hmong residents, who had been emigrating from Laos and refugee camps in Thailand since the end of the Vietnam War. The Hmong presence had considerable impact in LaCrosse; the public schools, in particular, needed to make efforts and adjustments in order to serve and incorporate this segment of the community. Following this description of the city and its residents, I will discuss the school district's busing plan including both the impetus for the plan and community reaction to it. As I have suggested, the busing plan was a subject of great debate and controversy as it was proposed and eventually implemented.

THE COMMUNITY OF LaCROSSE

LaCrosse is a city of about 50,000 residents in western Wisconsin. It is not a suburb of any larger city but, rather, is the largest city in a region of farms, small towns, and small cities. LaCrosse has a very picturesque setting, being situated between a line of high, rocky bluffs to the east and the Mississippi River to the west. Two other rivers, the LaCrosse and the Black, join the Mississippi here. The natural setting is important to LaCrosse's residents. Outdoor festivals and recreation are major parts of the city's communal life and also attract many tourists.

The city's economy at the time of this study was centered around small and midsize manufacturing firms and service providers, in addition to tourism. Among the largest employers were a brewery, a manufacturer of heating and cooling systems, two medical centers, the county government, the public school district, and the LaCrosse branch of the University of Wisconsin (*LaCrosse City Directory*, 1993). The unemployment rate was fairly low; in 1989 it was 6.2% among people 16 and over who were defined as members of the civilian labor force (U.S. Department of Commerce, 1992).

The median family household income in 1989 was $30,067. Around this median there was considerable variation: 19% of LaCrosse families had an income below $15,000, and 18% had an income above $50,000 (U.S. Department of Commerce, 1992).

The types of housing in LaCrosse span a broad range. Some of the grandest homes are three-story Victorian mansions built by lumber barons in the 1880s and 1890s. Also, there are newer subdivisions with expensive ranch-style houses. Within a few blocks of these, however, are homes —some owner-occupied and some rental properties—that are quite dilapidated. To someone accustomed to the layout of larger cities, cities of LaCrosse's size are striking for the geographic proximity of their wealthiest and poorest residents.

Prior to the early 1980s, LaCrosse's population was overwhelmingly White. With the influx of Hmong residents, the non-White population had grown by the early 1990s. At the time of the 1990 census, 94% of the city's 51,003 residents were White. About 5% were Asian or Pacific Islander, with four-fifths (about 2,000) of these people being Hmong. Blacks, Native Americans, and those classified as "other race" by the census bureau composed the remaining 1% of the population.

According to the 1990 census, 48,883 of LaCrosse's residents had been born in the United States; 77% of these had been born in the state of Wisconsin. Of the 2,120 foreign-born residents, over 70% had entered the United States since 1980 (U.S. Department of Commerce, 1992). This fact reflected the recent Hmong immigration.

The Hmong Population

Laotian Hmong immigrants began arriving in the United States in 1975 as refugees in the wake of the Vietnam and Indochina wars. During those wars, the Hmong supported the Royal Laotian government and its U.S.

allies in resisting the communist insurgent group known as the Pathet Lao (Chan, 1994). When the Pathet Lao gained control of Laos in 1975, the Hmong feared persecution. Many fled to Thailand for asylum. Between 1975 and 1990, more than 90,000 Laotian Hmong resettled in the United States, most by way of Thai refugee camps (Miyares, 1998; Trueba, Jacobs, & Kirton, 1990). The Hmong experience in America has received some attention from social scientists interested in the adaptation processes of immigrants and the communities that receive them (e.g., Hendricks, Downing, & Deinard, 1986; Hones, 1999a, 1999b; Hutchison & McNall, 1994; McNall, Dunnigan, & Mortimer, 1994; Rumbaut, 1989; Timm, 1994; Trueba, Cheng, & Ima, 1993).

In the early 1990s, the largest Hmong communities in the United States were in Fresno, California, and Minnesota's Twin Cities. Several Wisconsin cities also had Hmong populations of several thousand people. The initial immigrants to these cities often arrived through the sponsorships of local churches. More recently, immigration to these cities continued as the newly arriving Hmong sought to rejoin their kin networks.

In LaCrosse, there were approximately 2,600 Hmong residents in 1993 (*LaCrosse Tribune*, 1993f). While the flow of immigration had slowed, it had not ceased at the time of this study. English language skills and general adaptation to living in the United States varied among LaCrosse's Hmong. Most of the oldest Hmong spoke no English and would probably never learn the language. The people in their thirties and forties varied greatly in their English skills and their success in entering the labor force. A small number were employed in professional fields including law enforcement and education. Others had entered low-paying, unskilled jobs. Many were on welfare and were not employed. An estimated 65%–75% of Hmong in LaCrosse received public assistance. The *LaCrosse Tribune* (1994) reported that Wisconsin had the highest poverty rate in the nation for Asian children and that 72% of LaCrosse's Asian children lived in poverty.

Despite the hardships of poverty and refugee status, there seemed to be high aspirations and many successes among LaCrosse's Hmong students. High school graduation was an event that was celebrated by students and their families. From a group of Hmong in their teens and twenties featured in a special report in the *LaCrosse Tribune* (1993f), some entered college immediately after high school while others entered manufacturing or service jobs. Among the obstacles or competing lures that diminished the chance of completing secondary and postsecondary education were gang membership—a small but growing problem in LaCrosse—and Hmong traditions of early marriage and childbearing.

Research on the Hmong experience in other U.S. communities has shown that tensions arise in Hmong families as parents and grandparents struggle to balance their awareness of the importance of education for their children's success in American society with their fears of seeing traditional Hmong values, language, and culture weakened if their children embrace mainstream American attitudes and behaviors too vigorously (Chan, 1994; Hones, 1999a; Miyares, 1998). Relatedly, the family or extended clan remains central in determining the social structure and interpersonal relations of Hmong families (Chan, 1994; Miyares, 1998). Inasmuch as these issues can have implications for the ways Hmong children interact with others in school, they will be revisited later in this book.

The desegregation plan, which provides the context for this study, was never described by school district officials as an attempt at desegregating the district's Hmong students. Rather, it was described as an attempt at achieving socioeconomic balance among the district's elementary schools. But the enrollment growth and demographic changes that the LaCrosse school district experienced during the 1980s and early 1990s were driven largely by the Hmong immigration. And, indeed, the desegregation efforts did lessen the large concentrations of Hmong students in a few elementary schools.

THE DESEGREGATION PLAN

In order to serve an expanding enrollment, LaCrosse's public school district found it necessary to expand beyond its nine existing elementary schools by building two new ones prior to the 1992–93 school year. For a variety of reasons, the new schools were located on the outskirts of the city, and busing would be necessary to bring students to the schools.

The elementary school principals and other district administrators saw the necessity of new busing as an opportunity to desegregate the schools according to socioeconomic status. Among the nine previously operating elementary schools, there were great discrepancies in the student populations. In the whole district, approximately 1,300 of the 3,600 elementary school students (36%) received free or reduced-price lunches in 1992 (*Milwaukee Journal*, 1992a). Around this average, however, some schools had as many as 65%–70% of their students receiving free or reduced-price lunches; for others, the percentage was as low as 4% or 5%. Associated with these socioeconomic differences among the schools were marked differences in standardized test scores and in a variety of other measures.

The school board approved a busing plan that aimed at bringing each of the 11 schools (including the 2 newly built schools) within the range of 15%–45% of its students receiving free or reduced-price lunches. In introducing the plan to the public and to the media and in explaining the reasons for the desegregation efforts, district officials cited the value of diversity in the educational setting. The emphasis in public statements was upon the social benefits, rather than upon achievement measures such as standardized test scores.

An article in the *Milwaukee Journal*, appearing in January of 1992 (7 months before the new school boundaries took effect), quoted the district's business manager and two elementary school principals as follows:

> Business manager: "As long as that many children had to be moved anyway (to fill the new schools and lessen the overcrowding in other schools), we decided to see whether we could include a socioeconomic factor in the redistricting."

> First principal: "You need what we (at his school with a large concentration of low SES students) have to offer. Your children are going to be working in a society with far more diversity than the community you're living in right now."

> Second principal: "Other cities have allowed their ethnic enclaves to become hostile outposts. We have not yet built our walls of intolerance. LaCrosse has a chance to avoid that." (1992a, p. 5)

It is interesting to note that, while the district's official stance was always that the plan aimed at socioeconomic balance, the second principal's comments certainly imply concerns about ethnic or racial segregation. Other statements from district officials echoed the themes of the three quotations above. The main message seemed to be that socioeconomic balance in the schools would create a richer education environment that would enable children of diverse backgrounds to learn from each other (*Milwaukee Sentinel*, 1993).

Community Reaction to the Busing Plan

Considerable debate and protest arose at the time when the busing plan was announced and throughout the first year of the plan (*LaCrosse Tribune*, 1992a, 1992b, 1992c, 1992d, 1992e, 1992f, 1993a, 1993b, 1993c, 1993d, 1993e, 1993g, 1993h, 1993i, 1993j, 1993k; *Milwaukee Journal*, 1992b). The district announced the proposed changes in October 1991 and held three public forums to discuss them in November. At these forums, parents and other citizens offered various viewpoints: Some were enthusiastically in favor of the plan; others were angrily opposed.

In January of 1992, the school board voted 8 to 1 to approve the busing plan. Within a few weeks of the board's vote, a group calling itself the

Recall Alliance was formed. With about 16 leaders from the community, including an attorney, a doctor, and former and present city council members, the Recall Alliance called for replacing the school board and firing the superintendent and other district administrators.

Within a week of the Recall Alliance's formation, supporters of the school district organized, calling themselves the Coalition for Children. In the next weeks, Coalition and Alliance members held press conferences and engaged in heated debate. Those in favor of the plan praised its potential for teaching children to live with diversity. Those opposed to the plan called it an expensive and unwelcome experiment in social engineering. Further, opponents decried the shift away from neighborhood schools. In March, Alliance members began collecting signatures on petitions calling for a recall of the school board. In response to these petitions, Coalition members circulated petitions pledging support for the school district.

A general election in April, which was unrelated to the recall efforts, gave evidence of the public support for ousting incumbent school board members. In this general election, three challengers were voted into office, replacing three incumbents. Meanwhile, the recall efforts continued, as petitions were submitted to the school district calling for the six board members who had not been involved in the April election to face a recall vote.

Both personal animosity and legal challenges accompanied the submission of the petitions, and after some public shouting, shoving, and a judge's ruling, a recall election was held in July. Five challengers, all members of the Recall Alliance, were voted into office to replace five incumbents. A sixth challenger was slated to face a sixth incumbent in an August run-off election after neither candidate gained 51% of the votes in the July election in a three-person race for the incumbent's seat. This challenger withdrew from the race, however, saying she was disenchanted with the "foulness of political life" (*Milwaukee Journal*, 1992b).

The newly elected board members acted quickly with hopes of altering or eliminating the busing plan. In late July they invited David Armor, a sociologist and nationally known desegregation scholar, to speak at a public meeting about alternatives to the plan. Armor warned against forced busing as a means to desegregation and urged the district to consider voluntary means such as setting up magnet schools or establishing a parental choice program.

In fact, both the school board that was in place before the recall election and the board that was in place after the election, each in conjunction with district administrators, initiated some variations of parental choice to appease parents who were unhappy with their children's school assignments as dictated by the busing plan. However, only a small number of parents actually took advantage of the choice options.

With the beginning of the new school year upon them, the school board did not dismantle the busing plan. As the school year proceeded, much of the public criticism of the plan subsided, although the school board remained at odds with district administrators regarding the balance plan as well as other issues.

Widespread public support did not seem to stay with the school board members who were elected in the July 1992 recall election. In a general election in April 1993, three of these incumbents, who had been elected in the recall election, ran against three challengers. The challengers ousted the incumbents by fairly large margins of victory. The top vote-getter among the newly elected challengers was a Hmong man who strongly supported the balance plan. He and another man elected to the school board in Wausau, Wisconsin, on the same day were reported to be the first Hmong people in the state ever elected to public office.

CONCLUSION

This chapter has provided context for the rest of the book by describing LaCrosse and the socioeconomic balance plan that was initiated in its elementary schools at the start of the 1992–93 academic year. Although this balance plan was arguably a desegregation attempt, it differs from almost every other desegregation effort that has been tried and studied in the United States in the past few decades because the others have focused on racial divisions. The LaCrosse plan was always described as an attempt at mixing children from different socioeconomic backgrounds. Undeniably, though, the presence of both large Hmong and large White populations meant that race and ethnic culture were very salient issues in LaCrosse, as they have been in other desegregation settings.

Previous studies of desegregation and peer relations can offer insights and conceptualizations that are useful points of departure for this book. Turning to some of those studies, Chapter 2 primarily discusses research on organization, culture, and interpersonal relations within classrooms. And, as will be seen in this book's later chapters, this study is fundamentally based in the daily events and activities of 10 classrooms. In many regards, students' daily experiences were very much insulated from the community politics and dynamics described in this chapter. In other regards, however, one cannot fully understand the classrooms and schools without always remembering the larger context within which they were situated.

2

Desegregation, Integration, and the Gulf That Can Lie Between Them

Desegregation and integration are not the same phenomenon. Placing a diverse group of students together in one classroom may rate as a successful desegregation effort. However, many people will argue that successful integration has not been achieved until those students are relating to each other as social and intellectual equals—or at least until any status differences between students are unrelated to family income, race, or whatever else guided desegregation. The quality and extent of a school system's desegregation and integration depend on decisions and dynamics in the community, each school, and—ultimately—each classroom.

This chapter takes a step away from the specific events in LaCrosse to consider previous research and conceptualizations of desegregation and integration. This work is linked to sociological theories of small groups and reference groups. Next, useful perspectives and findings are drawn from studies of classroom organization and student stratification. This chapter thus provides concepts and perspectives that will serve as guides as the 10 LaCrosse classrooms are analyzed in subsequent chapters.

DESEGREGATION AND INTEGRATION

Virtually all existing research dealing with school desegregation and integration considers cases of racial desegregation. Although the present study investigates a school district that desegregated according to socioeconomic status, we can certainly learn from previous work. I follow other researchers in distinguishing between desegregation and integration (Berry, 1984; Cohen, 1984; Pettigrew, 1969; Schofield, 1982/1989, 1991, 1995; Slavin & Hansell, 1983). I define *desegregation* as a process by which the members of previously separated groups come into direct contact for at least some parts of their daily lives. I define *integration* as a process by which the members of previously status-differentiated groups come to interact as status equals in at least some parts of their daily lives. Each of the 10 classrooms described in this book was the product of desegregation efforts. Given that commonality, though, the classrooms varied in the degree to which they were integrated. Explaining that variation is a central goal of subsequent chapters.

The Contact Hypothesis

At least two distinct branches of research into school desegregation and integration can be identified. One branch discusses issues at the municipal, regional, or national level. Some of these studies have assessed the success of particular regions or districts in bringing about racial balance in schools (Coleman, Kelly, & Moore, 1975; Mills, 1979; Orfield & Eaton, 1996; Rivkin, 1994). Other studies discuss the role of desegregation in shaping race relations and attitudes toward liberalism and democracy (Hochschild, 1984; Olzak, Shanahan, & West, 1994).

A second branch of research, and the body of work more directly inspiring my study, deals with the daily events and interactions in schools and classrooms that are newly desegregated (Metz, 1978; Miller, 1983; Rist, 1978, 1979; Schofield, 1982/1989). A starting point for many studies within this second branch has been the *contact hypothesis*. An initial formulation of this hypothesis stated that one's behavior and attitudes toward members of a disliked social category will become more positive after direct interpersonal interaction with them (Miller & Brewer, 1984). In the 1940s and 1950s, however, qualifications were added to the contact hypothesis by Watson (1947), Williams (1947), Allport (1954), and others. These qualifications focused on the occurrence of contact under equal-status conditions as a necessity for improved intergroup behavior and attitudes. Specifically, in hypothesizing the conditions needed for improved intergroup relations, the following were stated (Cook, 1978; Miller & Brewer, 1984):

1. Contact must occur in circumstances that define the status of the participants of the two social groups as equal.
2. The attributes of members of the disliked group with whom the contact occurs must disconfirm the prevailing stereotyped beliefs about them.
3. The contact situation must encourage, or perhaps require, a mutually interdependent relationship, that is, cooperation in the achievement of a joint goal.

4. The contact situation must have high acquaintance potential; that is, it must promote association of the sort that reveals enough detail about the member of the disliked group to encourage seeing him or her as an individual rather than as a person with stereotyped group characteristics.
5. The social norms of the contact situation must favor group equality and egalitarian intergroup association.

Several things must be said about how the contact hypothesis relates to the present study. First, for most descriptions and analyses of the LaCrosse classrooms, I will focus on three groups: Asian American, high-SES non-Asian, and low-SES non-Asian. (Only one Asian American student in the study did not receive free or reduced-price lunches, which is my indicator of SES; thus there is not sufficient variation to consider both high- and low-SES Asian Americans.) The contact hypothesis has traditionally considered two groups. However, there are no unmanageable difficulties in studying the degree to which the members of three groups, rather than two, are interacting as status equals, as mutually interdependent actors, and as individuals.

A second issue is the nature of the initial relationship or sentiment between groups. The contact hypothesis traditionally assumes initial dislike between groups. In the 10 classrooms of my study, students who had not known each other previously probably did not approach one another with strong dislike in most cases. But while dislike was not prevalent, stereotypes about groups probably were prevalent. For instance, in the wake of LaCrosse's desegregation, it would have been quite apparent that particular classmates were arriving from a certain neighborhood or from another school. Among school children (as well as others), people from particular neighborhoods or schools are often stereotyped as being high achievers or low achievers, rich or poor, nice or snobbish. Thus, although I may not be studying the rate at which disliking turned to liking, I can inquire about the rate at which stereotypes gave way to more intimate, individualized relations.

Schofield (1982/1989) wrote about the shift from intergroup behavior to more interpersonal behavior. She and her collaborators observed Black and White students over the course of 3 years in a newly opened middle school, which had racial integration as a primary goal. While the transition was not complete after 3 years, Schofield noted that both Black and White students were more likely to relate to classmates as individuals rather than as members of racial in-groups or out-groups in the 2nd and 3rd years than they had been initially.

In the present study, it will be important to note the degree to which the condition of high acquaintance potential was met in each classroom; that is, it will be important to note the extent to which classroom activities promoted association of the sort that revealed enough detail to encourage the transition from relations based on stereotyped group characteristics to more individualized relations.

Finally, we must consider the definition of *equal-status contact*. It would be a very rare classroom in which all students displayed exactly the same rates of participation and garnered the same amounts and types of the teacher's attention. Certainly none of the 10 classrooms in my study can be described as such. This very rigid definition, however, is not the one I will use. Rather I will follow other researchers in saying that a classroom displays equal-status contact among its students if rates of participation and the amounts and types of attention received from the teacher are unrelated to socioeconomic status or race.

Researchers who have tested and modified the contact hypothesis as it relates to schools have investigated the degree to which different teaching styles and classroom task structures satisfy the five conditions listed above (Cohen, 1984; Cook, 1984; Rogers, Hennigan, Bowman, & Miller, 1984; Slavin & Hansell, 1983). Ample evidence exists to show that increased contact does not guarantee friendly and egalitarian relations between previously segregated groups. In fact, when educators do not make explicit efforts toward insuring that the groups interact as status equals, relations seem to deteriorate over time (Gerard & Miller, 1975). These previous studies have highlighted the wide variation possible in social relations in desegregated classrooms. Further, they have shown links between this variation and differences in teachers' practices and classroom organization. These findings complement, and gain support from, sociological theories of small groups.

Small-Group Theory Related to the Contact Hypothesis

George Homans hypothesized in *The Human Group* (1950/1992) that "if the frequency of interaction between two or more persons increases, the degree of their liking for one another will increase, and vice versa" (p. 112). This hypothesis is strikingly similar to the initial formulations of the contact hypothesis (without its subsequent qualifications). Both Homans's hypothesis and the initial formulation of the contact hypothesis ignored the implications of individuals' differing positions, roles, and ranks within a small group.

But Homans, of course, recognized the insufficiency of his supposition. Within just a few pages of its statement, he offered the following two passages:

We have conceptually isolated interaction and sentiment in order to investigate the relationship between the two, but in real social behavior interaction and sentiment cannot be isolated from the third element, activity. . . . Two persons that interact with one another tend to like one another only if the activities each carries on do not irritate the other too much. If either of them behaves in an irritating way, the mere fact of bringing them together, increasing their interaction, may increase negative rather than positive sentiments. (p. 116)

Interaction and friendliness are positively associated only if authority . . . does not enter the situation being considered. When two men are working together and one is the boss of the other . . . the interaction between them, required by the job they are doing together, may be frequent, and yet the superior and the subordinate will scarcely become friends. (p. 116)

The passages highlight two important points. First, in understanding the nature of the sentiments between members of a small group, one must consider the nature of the activities in which they are jointly engaged. Second, one must consider the differences in the members' positions, roles, and ranks within the group. I will discuss the impact of a group's activities later in this chapter when I discuss the social organization of the classroom. Now I want to consider the importance of position, role, and rank within the group by drawing upon theories developed by Robert Merton and Terence Hopkins.

Merton's (1968) *reference-group theory* posited that individuals use the norms and activities of groups as frames of reference as they compare and assess themselves and others. The theory has been applied to small groups, in which people are engaged in face-to-face interaction with contact being close enough for each group member to receive a distinct impression or perception of every other member. It has also been applied to situations in which people compare themselves to large aggregates or general status categories of which they may or may not be members.

For present purposes, I will focus on the small-group situation and, specifically, the situation in which interpersonal comparisons are limited to one's own small group. Merton (1968) asserted that for reference processes to take place a group must be characterized by at least a minimum degree of visibility. *Visibility* is defined as a group property; it is

the extent to which the structure of social organization provides occasion to those variously located in that structure to perceive the norms obtaining in the organization and the character of role-performance by those manning the organization. (p. 404)

Thus, visibility, as defined here, refers to the ability to see or perceive, conceptualized at the group level. The counterpart to visibility at the individual level is *observability*. Recognizing that there is variability among a group's members in their opportunities to observe the events and conditions of the group, it is useful to define this individual property as being subtly distinct from visibility. Observability, then, is the individual's opportunity to observe the norms of the group and the actions of other members of the group.

Hopkins (1964) used Merton's concept of observability to develop a model in which "rank is seen to lead to centrality, centrality to observability and conformity, these to influence, then influence back to rank, and so on" (p. 8). Here *rank* is defined as the generally agreed-upon worth or standing of a group member relative to other members. *Centrality* refers simultaneously to the frequency with which a member interacts with other members and the number or range of other members with whom he or she interacts. *Observability* is defined as I have defined it above and involves the ability to observe or perceive norms and others' actions. *Conformity* is the congruence between a member's profile on the relevant norms and the profile of group-held norms. *Influence* is defined as the effect of a member's actions on the group's normative consensus.

Ultimately in this study of LaCrosse's classrooms, I am interested in the nominations students received as being desirable workmates and playmates. These nominations give a good indication of each student's rank within the classroom. Hopkins's model will be useful in guiding the investigation. The concepts of visibility and observability will be especially relevant in regard to the ways classroom organization and teachers' practices affect the structure of peer relations because these are probably the concepts in Hopkins' model most directly affected by task structures, disciplinary practices, and other aspects of classroom organization.

Hopkins's model offers insights into the differences in group members' positions and ranks in the group. The importance of recognizing these differences was illustrated by the modifications to Homans's initial hypothesis and qualifications of the contact hypothesis. The concepts of visibility and observability will be of particular interest in the following chapters. Differences between the 10 classrooms in the level of visibility afforded to students will be linked to patterns of peer relations in each classroom. Differences within each classroom in the level of observability characterizing each student will be linked to each individual's rank and popularity.

Finally, a third concept will prove useful. This might be called *observedness* and refers to the degree to which an individual's behaviors and attitudes can be perceived by other members of the group. Like observability, observedness is a concept at the individual level. Also like observability, an individual's observedness—in conjunction with his or her attitudes and behaviors—can be linked to his or her rank and popularity.

SOCIAL ORGANIZATION OF THE CLASSROOM

Throughout this book, I will be investigating the extent to which classroom activities, reward structures, and teacher leadership styles affected the LaCrosse students' opportunities to see and be seen, to speak and be heard, to be chosen or not chosen as friends and workmates. Featured activities, reward structures, and leadership styles are contextual variables that are affected by adults' conscious decisions or subconscious predilections. As such, they can be expected to vary among classrooms. Furthermore, they largely determine the extent to which the five conditions hypothesized as necessary for improved intergroup relations (listed earlier in this chapter) are realized. The investigation of these classroom characteristics and their effects upon peer relations and participation can be guided by some useful perspectives and insights from studies of the social organization of the classroom.

Research in this field has considered the impact of the ways teachers divide students into learning groups (Barr & Dreeben, 1983; Slavin & Oickle, 1981), task and reward structures (Bossert, 1979; Marshall & Weinstein, 1984), and various disciplinary styles (Bidwell, 1965; Metz, 1978; Waller, 1932). Much of this research has considered the ways social organization of the classroom affects the level and distribution of achievement outcomes (e.g., grades and test scores). Given the focus of this book, I want to give special attention to research that has also considered effects on friendships, affiliations, and participation.

Applications to Peer Relations and Participation

Studies of classroom processes show that teachers' decisions about instructional activities and modes of discipline and control have strong implications for the ways students experience the schooling process. Allocation of resources, including a teacher's time and attention, affects each student's social and academic development. Peer relations and participation in classroom activities are integral parts of both social and academic development.

Bossert's (1979) study of third- and fourth-grade classrooms illustrates how the organization of instructional activities affects the social relationships that develop within classrooms. His research demonstrated a chain of events by which the type of task organization employed affects the type of authority used by the teacher, the allocation of assistance to students, and emerging peer relations. Specifically, in Bossert's observations, whole-class instruction and recitation were associated with impartial and impersonal means of controlling pupils. Somewhat paradoxically, however, these types of task organization or instructional style were also associated with relying on top performers to answer the majority of questions and to serve as models for the rest of the class. Friendship groupings in classrooms characterized by recitation and whole-class instruction tended to form among children who were performing at similar levels.

Bossert explained the patterns he observed in classrooms focused on whole-class instruction by noting the fragility of classroom order and the flow of instruction when an entire class was engaged in a common activity. In this setting, an angry or restless child could easily disrupt instruction for the entire class. Wishing to maintain the flow of activities, teachers tended to respond to disruptions with disciplinary actions that were as brief as possible. Also, because of the very public atmosphere of whole-class instruction, teachers knew that the rest of the class would be watching as any student was disciplined. Hence, teachers were very cognizant of treating all students in a standardized fashion, not varying responses student by student.

Finally, the tendency of teachers to call most often on the stronger academic performers was another attempt to maintain the pace of activities, as these students' correct responses helped to move the class along. In classrooms using whole-class recitation, students were all engaged in a common task, performing in front of one another. As a result, the general social climate of these classrooms was very competitive and achievement-oriented, producing a social hierarchy based on achievement, and causing stable friendships to develop primarily among children who were performing at similar academic levels.

In contrast, Bossert described a set of classrooms which were characterized by multitask organization. In these classrooms, different individuals or small groups would typically be working on a varied assortment of projects. Pupils who excelled at a particular task were expected to help others or to work independently, leaving the teacher free to assist those pupils having the most difficulty.

Teachers in multitask classrooms tended to use more personalistic means of control. They could tailor disciplinary responses to the needs of individual children because, as students were engaged in their individual work or small-group projects, all eyes were not upon the handling of an angry or restless child. More time could be taken with disciplining or assisting individuals who seemed to need the most attention because the whole class did not have to wait while the teacher dealt privately with one student. In multitask classrooms, task performance was (1) less visible than in recitation or whole-class settings, (2) largely independent of others' performance, and (3) noncomparable. Apparently as a result, peer relations were less affected by students' academic achievement. Instead, students tended to form relatively fluid friendships based on current common interests.

A study by Hallinan and Tuma (1978) provides more evidence of the effect of task structure and classroom organization on friendship patterns. Using longitudinal sociometric data from fourth-, fifth-, and sixth-grade students, these researchers investigated the impact of (1) opportunities for pairs of students to interact (as measured by whether the students had the same reading teacher and the percentage of instructional time spent in small groups), (2) task homogeneity within small groups (when considering two students in the same group), (3) topic and material homogeneity between small instructional groups (when considering two students in different groups), and (4) students' freedom to determine the membership of their reading groups.

With an increase in each measure or set of measures (1 through 4, above), Hallinan and Tuma hypothesized that friendships would become more friendly. For example, high proportions of instructional time spent in small groups were hypothesized to be positively associated with pairs of students reporting an upgrading of their friendship status as the school year progressed from "non-friend" to "friend" or from "friend" to "best friend." Conversely, high proportions of instructional time spent in small groups were hypothesized to be negatively associated with students reporting a downgrading of their friendship status as the year progressed. Further, an increase in each measure or set of measures was expected to be positively associated with the stability of strong friendships (i.e., best friends remaining best friends as the year progressed). Fairly strong support was shown for the hypotheses, with weak friendships being influenced by classroom features more often than strong friendships were.

Another study by Hallinan (1979) contrasted traditional classrooms with open classrooms. In the traditional classrooms, students were assigned to seats; instructional groups were determined by the teacher. In open classrooms, students were permitted to select their own seating arrangements and instructional groups and, in general, were freer to move about the classroom. Contrary to Hallinan's original hypotheses, the open classrooms were characterized by fewer "best friendships," fewer cross-sex friendships, and more social isolates. In offering a post hoc explanation, Hallinan suggested that students took advantage of their freedom of choice to avoid becoming friendly with peers who were unlikely to reciprocate their friendship or with members of the opposite sex or unpopular children when such choices would violate group norms. Further, Hallinan suggested that teachers in traditional classrooms were able to use their power to assign seats and work areas in order to encourage friendships between students who might otherwise avoid one another.

Cone and Perez's (1986) study of the impact of seating arrangements and other aspects of a classroom's physical layout adds support to Hallinan's gender results. Cone and Perez's principal finding was that elementary school students used their freedom to choose seats and organize classroom space to create single-sex territories. In this way, boys' and girls' same-sex friendships were reinforced by the physical layout that teachers permitted and students helped create.

Finally, Slavin and Oickle (1981) provided further evidence of the impact of classroom organization on friendship patterns with their investigation of the effects of cooperative learning teams on cross-racial friendships in a desegregated middle school that served Black and White students. Cooperative learning environments, in which students worked in small, heterogeneous teams to master academic materials, were compared with control classrooms, in which the same curricular materials were covered at the same pace but without cooperative teams. A marginally significant positive relationship was found between the cooperative setting and cross-racial friendships, with the effect being disproportionately due to White students gaining Black friends.

In comparing Bossert's work to the other four studies—Hallinan and Tuma's, Hallinan's, Cone and Perez's, and Slavin and Oickle's—one can see an important feature of Bossert's work that is absent in the others. Bossert explicitly described the fact that particular modes of task organization lend themselves to particular modes of teacher authority and discipline. Different modes of task organization, authority, and discipline, in turn, provide different levels of visibility in the classroom as students form opinions and assessments of themselves and others.

The main variation in disciplinary styles that Bossert described was the contrast between the universalistic style predominant in recitation settings and the particularistic style predominant in multitask settings. *Universalism* involves holding all students to the same standards, and treating them alike in response to given actions or behaviors. *Particularism* involves varying standards, expectations, or treatment of individuals student-by-student, often in response to the context of a given situation and the characteristics of the students involved.

The contrast between universalism and particularism has received much attention (Bidwell, 1965; Dreeben, 1968; Parsons, 1951, 1959). There is a fundamental tension between a teacher's motivations to implement each of the two styles. And, as Bossert (1979) and Metz (1986/1992) have stressed, the selection of one task structure or another largely determines the direction in which the balance will tip. The resultant classroom atmosphere has strong implications for the relationship between teacher and student and for relationships among students.

Bossert's work developed the idea that a teacher's leadership style affects students' public displays and, consequently, the status system among students. Further development of this idea has been offered by Susan Rosenholtz, Elizabeth Cohen, Carl Simpson, and several of their colleagues (Cohen & Lotan, 1995, 1997; Rosenholtz, 1982; Rosenholtz & Cohen, 1983; Rosenholtz & Rosenholtz, 1981; Rosenholtz & Simpson, 1984; Rosenholtz & Wilson, 1980; Simpson, 1981).

Among the most important findings to come from this line of inquiry is evidence about the "dimensionality" of classroom organization, and its effects on students' perceptions of their ability and the ability of others (Rosenholtz & Simpson, 1984). Cohen (1997) summarized some of the research on two contrasting types of classrooms—unidimensional and multidimensional—as follows:

> Unidimensional organization of instruction establishes conditions that facilitate "ability formation." In unidimensional classrooms, daily activities encourage comparison and imply a single underlying dimension of comparison. When instruction and student performances imply few performance dimensions, students' perceptions of ability become one-dimensional.
>
> The first feature of unidimensional classrooms is an undifferentiated task structure. All students work on similar tasks or with a narrow range of materials and methods. For example, unidimensional classes require reading for successful performance of most tasks and rely mostly on paper-and-pencil tasks. This task structure facilitates social comparison; students can easily tell how well they are doing in comparison to others. A second feature of unidimensional classrooms is a low level of student autonomy, reducing the variety of tasks and preventing students from using their own evaluations of performance. Third, unidimensional classrooms use whole class instruction or clear-cut ability groups. A final feature is the emphasis on grading to convey clear-cut, unidimensional evaluation by teachers.
>
> In contrast, the multidimensional classroom has varied materials and methods, a higher degree of student autonomy, more individual tasks, varied grouping patterns, and less reliance on grading. In a comparison of these two types of classrooms, researchers have found that students' self-reported ability levels have a greater variance in unidimensional classrooms (Rosenholtz & Rosenholtz, 1981; Simpson, 1981). In multidimensional classrooms, fewer children define themselves as "below average," thus restricting the distribution of self-evaluations. Student reports of peers' ability levels are also more dispersed and more consensual . . . in unidimensional classes, and perceptions of individual ability are much more closely related to ratings by teachers and peers. (p. 8)

There are many parallels between the whole-class recitation classrooms described by Bossert and the unidimensional classrooms described here. Both are characterized by very public and visible performance. Both engender rigid status hierarchies and friendship groupings closely tied to students' performance on a narrow range of academic criteria. There are also parallels between Bossert's multitask settings and multidimensional classrooms, including less visible task performance and less rigid and consensual hierarchy in student reports of ability levels and social standing.

Cohen and her colleagues have been concerned about the ways traditional classroom structure—including the ubiquitous unidimensional classroom—reinforces inequities commonly associated with race and socioeconomic status. These inequities reveal themselves in student perceptions of their own and classmates' abilities, in friendship choices, in classroom participation, and in student achievement.

Consequently, attempts have been made to change classroom organization in order to alter "expectations for competence," minimize classroom stratification, and promote equal-status interaction among students. Cohen and Lotan (1995, 1997) provide evidence that two particular strategies to be used in conjunction with cooperative small-group tasks are effective in meeting these goals. These strategies are (1) orienting students toward a multiple-ability perspective and (2) publicly assigning competence to traditionally low-status students. Developing a multiple-ability orientation among students "is grounded in the use and analysis of multiple-ability tasks and is based on the teacher's public recognition of the wealth of intellectual abilities that are relevant and valued in the classroom, just as they are in daily life" (Lotan, 1997, p. 23). Assigning competence to low-status students occurs during the course of group activities as a teacher pays particular attention to low- status students and watches for instances when they show noteworthy competence on a task. The teacher then tells these students what they did well and how their contributions were relevant to the group endeavor. Further, the teacher generally points out to the group how these students can serve as resources on a similar task in the future (Lotan, 1997).

While these are two very specific classroom strategies, they are based upon more general principles. They seek to expand the range of featured and rewarded activities in the classroom, and they seek to weaken the grip of rigid status hierarchies based on a narrow range of student abilities or characteristics. In doing so, they are consistent with the five conditions hypothesized as necessary for improved intergroup relations, which were listed earlier in this chapter. Specifically, these classroom strategies aim to equalize the status of a classroom's members, to disconfirm stereotyped beliefs about traditionally low-status students, to increase acquaintance potential by displaying a wide range of individuals' talents and interests, and to promote equality and egalitarian relations. Furthermore, because they are used within a cooperative learning environment, they clearly require mutual interdependence among students in pursuit of a joint goal.

CONCLUSION

This chapter has highlighted some concepts that will be important throughout the remainder of this book in the consideration of peer relations and participation in the LaCrosse classrooms. These include desegregation, integration, equal-status contact, a classroom's task structure, the range of featured and rewarded topics and activities, a teacher's disciplinary style, and the degree of visibility under which students see one another perform academically and socially. With these concepts as guides, it is time to step inside the five schools and 10 classrooms that are at the heart of this study.

3

Places and Cases: The Toolbox Opened

When I learned of the events in LaCrosse through newspaper and television reports in the summer of 1992, the main question that interested me as a researcher was this: Even when a school district is successful in achieving desegregation, will this imply true integration? That is, would students' friendships and affiliations in these LaCrosse schools cross lines of socio-economic status (SES), neighborhood, and race? If the answer was "yes, sometimes," I wanted to study the conditions that facilitate integration and the conditions that inhibit integration.

I was able to gain access for my research at the beginning of the 2nd year of the busing plan (at the beginning of the 1993–94 school year). It would have been preferable to begin the study in the spring or fall of 1992, but, for a variety of reasons, that was not possible. Nonetheless, even in the 2nd year, new patterns of interaction, new friendships and affiliations were likely to be forming. And in retrospect, the data make it clear that this 2nd year of desegregation was still a year of change and emergence of social relations.

I used a combination of qualitative and quantitative data to address my questions. The main sources are (1) three spans of observation in each of the 10 classrooms, (2) interviews with teachers, and (3) sociometric measures of students' friendships and affiliations.

In this chapter, I introduce the five schools in my study, each of which experienced a unique set of changes in the wake of the desegregation plan. This variation allows me to address important questions about the ways students' enrollment paths and the composition of students in a classroom interact with a teacher's style and the social organization of the classroom in influencing peer relations and participation. Each of the various data sources, as I explain in the second part of this chapter, contributes to our understanding of classroom organization, peer relations, and participation in desegregated classrooms.

SELECTION OF FIVE SCHOOLS AND TEN CLASSROOMS

The first step in the research design was to select the exact population to be studied. Individual classrooms were necessarily the primary unit of analysis given my research agenda. Considering the type of observation I wanted to do, I thought I could study 8–10 classrooms. I decided that all of the classrooms should serve the same grade; I did not want to add age or developmental maturity as variables in addition to the many other relevant factors I would need to consider.

I chose fourth-grade classrooms for two reasons. First, I reasoned that fourth-grade students would be old enough to answer the questions of my sociometric instrument. Second, because LaCrosse's elementary schools served kindergarten through fifth grade, most of the study's participants would still be at the same schools in the year after my fieldwork in case any follow-up contacts were necessary.

I decided that studying two classrooms per school would give me some ability to discern when emerging patterns were associated with the school setting and when emerging patterns were associated with the characteristics of particular teachers and classrooms. After consulting with some of the district's principals and other administrators, I selected 5 of the district's 11 elementary schools as my research sites: New Forest, Campus Edge, Fawndale, Riverside, and Maple Grove Elementary Schools. Each of the 5 had experienced a unique transition in the wake of the busing plan.

New Forest

New Forest Elementary School was one of the two schools that were newly opened for the 1992–93 school year. This school was of particular interest because the setting was new to all students and teachers at the inception of the busing plan; no one could claim the school as "old turf."

New Forest was located at the edge of the city and almost every student arrived by bus or car pool. The new attendance zones implemented for the 1992–93 school year determined that New Forest would draw students from what were previously the attendance zones of four different schools. Additionally, due to students moving within or from outside the district, New Forest had students who previously had attended schools other than those four.

The New Forest student body was split quite evenly between students who received free or reduced-price lunches and students who did not. Table 3.1 shows the school's percentage of low-SES students (those who received free or reduced-price lunches) during the 1992–93 school year. During the

Table 3.1. Percentage of students in all LaCrosse elementary schools
receiving free or reduced-price lunch in the year before and the year
after the initiation of the desegregation plan

School	1991–92	1992–93
New Forest	---	50
Campus Edge	23	32
Fawndale	68	43
Maple Grove	13	22
Riverside	7	19
Non-Study School #1	32	41
Non-Study School #2	68	63
Non-Study School #3	18	24
Non-Study School #4	18	24
Non-Study School #5	4	21
Non-Study School #6	---	29

Source: School district of LaCrosse, as reported in the *Milwaukee Sentinel* (1993)

year of my field work, the composition of the student body remained similar
to that of the previous year.

In general, I noticed a strong emphasis on developing unity and community at New Forest. There were at least three interrelated reasons for
this emphasis. First, the personalities and educational philosophies of the
staff, most notably the principal, encouraged unity. Various conversations
led me to believe that the New Forest staff was recruited by district administrators with the intention of assembling a group dedicated to building social bonds and integration among New Forest students.

Second, the school's remote location and the diversity of the student
body made the obstacles to school spirit and integration especially
apparent. The staff seemed to perceive these obstacles and to place a
high priority on addressing them. An example of the staff's responsive-
ness to obstacles was described to me by Mrs. Nash, one of the fourth
grade teachers.

Mrs. Nash described an outdoor carnival that had been held for students and their families on a weekend afternoon during the 1992–93 school
year. On the following Monday, Mrs. Nash mentioned to a Hmong boy in
her class that she had seen his brother and sister at the carnival, but not
him. She wondered why. He explained that there was not enough room
for everybody in the family's car so he had stayed home. (His was a large

family.) In response to situations like this, Mrs. Nash said that thereafter, whenever an evening or weekend event was scheduled, students were told that arrangements could be made if they did not have a ride or a way to get to the school.

Finally, there was a third likely reason for the New Forest staff's emphasis on community building. Because New Forest was one of the two schools that were new to the district in the 1st year of the desegregation plan, there seemed to be some sense that the eyes of the district and the community were on the school to see whether the plan was "working." In conversations with me, teachers and parents from other schools were interested in any ways that I might see New Forest as being different from their schools. These teachers and parents seemed to accept the two new schools as being fundamentally different from the other schools. They seemed to perceive the new schools as being the places where the district's mixing, experimenting, and commitment to integration were at their greatest. To the extent that the New Forest staff were aware of these perceptions, or shared them, the staff might have redoubled their efforts toward building community and cohesion.

Many events during my visits at New Forest convinced me of the staff's commitment to community building. One especially poignant example was a bus meeting I watched. These meetings were scheduled monthly for the first part of the school year, and later, somewhat less frequently. At each meeting approximately 45 minutes were allocated for the students from each school bus to meet with two teachers and their bus driver. The two teachers had the yearlong responsibility of escorting students to the bus after school, maintaining daily contact with the driver, and dealing with behavior problems.

Meetings such as these, and the invitation for the bus drivers to visit the classrooms, were events I did not witness or hear about at any of the other schools I visited. At the meetings, students were asked to discuss things that had happened during the trips to and from New Forest and to suggest things that could make their buses better. The drivers were encouraged by the teachers to join the discussion. The drivers seemed somewhat uneasy and were not as articulate as the teachers. The drivers' very presence, however, seemed to me to capture perfectly the effort made by the New Forest principal and staff to integrate every member of the school community and to communicate to students that respect should be accorded to people from all walks of life. As will be seen in subsequent chapters, the staff's philosophies and efforts did not necessarily translate into what would be called complete integration, but the depiction presented above is central to what the reader should keep in mind when New Forest is discussed further.

Campus Edge

Campus Edge Elementary School was located in a middle-class residential neighborhood, on the edge of the campus of the local branch of the state university. Prior to the desegregation plan, Campus Edge served a relatively advantaged population, although there was certainly some diversity in the socioeconomic circumstances of the student body. In the year before the desegregation plan, approximately 23% of Campus Edge students received free or reduced-price lunches, while the other 77% did not.

The most dramatic implication of the desegregation plan for Campus Edge was that students living within an area of approximately 50 contiguous city blocks who previously had attended Campus Edge were assigned to attend Fawndale Elementary School beginning with the 1992–93 school year. Other students who previously had attended Campus Edge were assigned to New Forest. These reassigned students were almost exclusively from high-SES homes. Some of the parents affected by this reassignment were among those who had voiced their opposition to the busing plan most adamantly. Some of those opposed to the reassignment were granted transfers back to Campus Edge. A few others enrolled their children in parochial schools. Most enrolled their students in the newly assigned schools in accordance with the desegregation plan.

In addition to the departure of these high-SES students, some low-SES students were newly assigned to Campus Edge through the desegregation plan. These students did not move to Campus Edge with large numbers of their former schoolmates. Rather, a few students in each grade were reassigned to Campus Edge from other schools. As a result of the new attendance zones, for the 1992–93 school year 32% of Campus Edge students received free or reduced-price lunches while the other 68% did not.

Regarding Campus Edge's climate and organizational characteristics, two factors struck me as contrasting sharply with the other schools. First, this was the school with the most direct and influential parental involvement. Second, this was the school in which the principal was least likely to monitor a teacher's activities or to visit a classroom.

My first evidence of the high level of parental involvement came when I requested permission to include Campus Edge in the study. At each of the other four schools, either the principal had decided unilaterally that his or her school would participate, or the decision was made by the principal in consultation with the two teachers who would be involved. At Campus Edge, in contrast, the principal explained to me that a model of shared decision making was followed. I was asked to prepare written materials for the members of a committee comprising parents, teachers, and other school staff. Only after I had met with this committee and gained their approval was I able to finalize my plans with the two teachers at Campus Edge. This committee met regularly during the school year and had a part in making many decisions about the school.

Further evidence of the high degree of parental involvement, or at least parents' desire for a high degree of involvement, was apparent throughout the school year. It was common to see parents visiting the classrooms at Campus Edge before or after school. It was common for a parent to come to the classroom to get homework if his or her child had stayed home with an illness. At none of the five schools in the study was it uncommon for parents to visit a classroom, but it seemed to happen most often at Campus Edge. There also seemed to be a steady supply of eager parent volunteers to help at the school or chaperone field trips. Some parents, in comments written on surveys I collected, expressed dissatisfaction that there were not more opportunities for involvement at the school.

Regarding the principal's role, Campus Edge's principal seemed to have less frequent contact with teachers than did the other four principals in the study, and he was not as likely as the others to visit a classroom. This situation meant that the teachers had a lot of autonomy in organizing their classrooms; it also contributed to the sense that each of the classrooms was a fairly self-contained unit. In contrast, at New Forest, Maple Grove, and Riverside there seemed to be more interaction among each school's fourth-grade classrooms in terms of teachers planning teaching units jointly or classes being combined for certain lessons or activities. The hands-off role played by Campus Edge's principal also meant that the Campus Edge teachers were unlikely to send misbehaving students to the school office for discipline, whereas the principals at Riverside, Fawndale, and Maple Grove were quite likely to take a lead role in discipline.

Fawndale

Fawndale Elementary School was located in a working-class neighborhood in a fairly old residential district. A lot of low-SES Hmong students and low-SES White students lived close to the school. Prior to the desegregation plan, approximately 68% of Fawndale's students received free or reduced-price lunches.

With the busing plan, some students who had previously attended Fawndale were bused to other schools, including New Forest and Riverside. Also, a large group of former Campus Edge students was newly assigned to Fawndale. As mentioned above, some of the Campus Edge parents requested and were granted transfers for their children back to Campus Edge, and a few others enrolled their children in parochial schools rather than at Fawndale. Most, however, enrolled their children at Fawndale in accordance with the district's plan. In the 1st year of the busing plan, approximately 43% of Fawndale's students received free or reduced-price lunches.

Fawndale is interesting in comparison with the other schools in the study because it was a location at which most of the low-SES students were on their "own turf" when a group of high-SES students newly arrived in the wake of the desegregation plan. Would the low-SES students at Fawndale set the normative tone and hold positions of prestige and centrality in ways that low-SES students at other schools did not? Or would Fawndale's newly arrived high-SES students establish themselves as normative exemplars and central, popular students by virtue of valued and rewarded behaviors and abilities? For the most part, I will let the answers to questions like these reveal themselves gradually in the coming chapters.

Some details about the climate at Fawndale in the wake of the busing plan are informative, however. First, the school retained an awareness of the domestic problems facing many of its students living near Fawndale, such as alcohol and drug abuse, domestic violence, and youth delinquency. Upon entering the school, one saw a table and bulletin board providing information about various social service providers.

Second, during the 2nd year of the busing plan, many of the parents and students who were new to Fawndale still seemed to be in the process of establishing patterns of participation at the school and links between home and school. There was an ambivalence about how much time and energy some of the parents who were new to Fawndale would invest in the school and in their children's new classmates. In responding to my questionnaire, a couple of the parents whose children had previously attended Campus Edge stated that they were concerned about some of the behavior displayed and language used by students at Fawndale. These parents said they were willing to leave their children at Fawndale for another year, but remained cautious.

One of Fawndale's teachers told me that some of the parents whose children had previously attended Campus Edge had organized a couple of roller-skating parties for Fawndale students. Because the roller-skating rink was nearer to Campus Edge than to Fawndale and because communication about the first of these parties was poor, very few of the students who lived near Fawndale attended the first party. The teacher who told me about this situation felt that it had been somewhat divisive for students. For the second roller-skating party, however, communication about the event was better, and some of the parents who were organizing the party offered to drive students who lived near Fawndale. The teacher felt that this second party had been more successful and better for the school community.

Riverside

Riverside Elementary School gained some low-SES students with the busing plan. What distinguishes Riverside and Maple Grove (described below) from the others—from New Forest and Fawndale, especially—is that students who were new to Riverside and Maple Grove arrived in relative isolation. That is, they did not enter their new schools with large numbers of their former classmates.

Riverside was located on an island just west of LaCrosse in a small township served by the LaCrosse school district. The island was situated at the confluence of the Mississippi River and a smaller river that flows from the east. The residential areas surrounding the school were not especially affluent, but the 7% of students receiving free or reduced-price lunches before the desegregation plan was the second-lowest percentage in the district. With the plan's new attendance zones, some low-SES students were newly assigned to Riverside. In the first year of the plan, 19% of Riverside's students received free or reduced-price lunches.

Even before the desegregation plan, however, Riverside served students from many neighborhoods because the school served many of the district's students with severe emotional problems, behavioral problems, or learning disabilities. The students with special needs generally spent the first few minutes and the last few minutes of each school day in a *mainstream*, or regular, classroom. Additionally, except for those with the most severe disabilities, these students joined their mainstream classes for music, art, gym, lunch, and recess. Otherwise, the mainstream teachers and the special education teachers decided on a student-by-student basis how much of the rest of the school day each student with special needs should spend in his or her mainstream classroom. This amount of time varied from none to an hour or more.

Recess on the playground at Riverside was a time when the social divisions between the students with special needs and the school's other students were very apparent. The common pattern was for the fourth-grade students with special needs to play dodgeball or basketball in a group, often joined by a small number of other students who were not readily accepted by the rest of their classmates. The majority of fourth-grade boys would play kickball or football in one or two groups, while the majority of fourth-grade girls played tag or played on the playground equipment in smaller groups. The students with special needs were ignored for the most part by the majority of students, and vice versa.

In subsequent chapters, when sociometric data are discussed, it will be apparent that students with special needs were almost never named as desired workmates or daily playmates by their mainstream classmates. I am able to account quite well for any workmate and playmate nominations directed toward these students. Unfortunately, though, because I was not very successful in collecting sociometric data from students with special needs, I am able to provide only limited analyses of *their* preferences.

Riverside's setting on an island with considerable wildlife provided interesting educational opportunities. In the discussion of the two Riverside classrooms, it will be seen that tallies of eagle sightings, walks to the "frog pond" in search of flora and fauna, and measurement lessons conducted in snow drifts were parts of these fourth-grade students' learning and interaction. The teachers of both of the classrooms I visited worked quite closely and very well with Riverside's principal. He was a principal who offered ready support to his teachers in disciplining and counseling students and in communicating with parents. His approach to the varied needs of Riverside's students was shared by the two teachers: All three seemed to place a high priority on knowing well each student's strengths, weaknesses, proclivities, and problems.

Interestingly, however, there were limits to how particularistic the Riverside teachers and principal were toward students. To a considerable degree, they seemed to keep their individualized treatment of students behind the scenes. Regarding behavior, if not achievement, in the more public moments of instruction and discipline, students received the impression that all were expected to follow the same rules and meet the same standards. More particularistic considerations were reserved for the less public moments of deciding which students should join a mainstream classroom, which students required conferences or discipline, and how to structure lessons and classroom activities to reach all students.

Maple Grove

Maple Grove Elementary School was located in a middle-class neighborhood. The school gained some low-SES students with the implementation of the busing plan; also some high-SES students were moved from Maple Grove to other schools. In the year before the plan, 13% of Maple Grove's students received free or reduced-price lunches. In the first year of the plan, 22% received free or reduced-price lunches. Although some new students came to the school because of the busing plan, these students did not arrive in large numbers and were not accompanied by large numbers of former schoolmates.

Maple Grove had the feel of a very traditional elementary school. In fact, Maple Grove and its classrooms were the settings that most reminded me of my own fourth-grade experiences in 1978. The principal was visible in leading school assemblies, in overseeing discipline, and in communicating with parents. He visited classrooms on occasion, but seemed to give teachers a lot of freedom to organize and conduct their classes. The teachers I visited, as I will describe in the next chapter, adhered to teaching techniques and philosophies that had guided them through several decades of teaching. In many ways, these were the teachers and the school that seemed to be conducting business as usual, with few adaptations or concessions prompted by the desegregation plan.

DATA SOURCES

A combination of qualitative and quantitative data was collected to study two classrooms at each of the five schools. In this section, I will describe each of the main sources of data in more detail: (1) three spans of observation in each classroom, (2) interviews with teachers, and (3) sociometric measures of students' friendships and affiliations. In addition to these three data sources, I also administered two surveys to parents. These questionnaires asked for background information about parents and students. They also asked about parents' attitudes about their child's school, attitudes about the desegregation plan, parents' volunteering, and participation in school-related matters. Because completion rates for the two surveys were low (54% and 48%), these data are used only to supplement the other information sources.

Three Spans of Observation in Each Classroom

For each classroom, the observation entailed 2 or 3 complete school days at each of three points during the school year. The first period of observation was in September or October. The second was in January or February. The third was in April or May. In addition to observing in the classroom, I accompanied the students to lunch, recess, art, music, gym, and school assemblies whenever possible. My goal during most of the observation time was to be a silent, unobtrusive observer. During lunch, recess, and break times in the classroom, however, my interactions with the students and teacher were much more informal and participatory in nature.

Interviews with Teachers

The interviews were conducted in January and February. I asked the teachers about their instructional philosophies and techniques, their contact with parents, their attitudes toward the desegregation plan, and their perceptions of the plan's consequences. Of the 10 interviews, 8 followed a prepared protocol and were tape-recorded and transcribed. Interviews with the other two teachers consisted of a subset of the protocol's questions being asked during the course of other conversations; loose transcriptions of those responses were made. Of course, in addition to the interviews, many comments from the teachers at other points during the year provided insight into their teaching styles and philosophies. These comments were recorded in my observational notes.

Sociometric Measures of Students' Friendships and Affiliations

The sociometric measures include students' reports of friends they played with at recess, two classmates they would enjoy working with on a science project, classmates who had been to their homes, and their participation in extracurricular activities. The data collection was accomplished through a simple, open-ended questionnaire, which the students completed while I orally read and explained each item. (See Appendix.)

I collected these measures in the 5th week of the school year and again late in the school year (in April or May), which allows for the examination of change. Questionnaires were collected from all students in the 10 classrooms, except for a small number whose parents requested that the students not participate. Of the 227 students enrolled in the fall, I gathered sociometric data from 201. In the spring, after some students had moved into or out of the classes, 213 were enrolled, and I gathered sociometric data from 194.

Each student's nominations of preferred workmates (i.e., two classmates he or she would enjoy working with on a science project) will be central to this book's analyses. It is reasonable to ask about the implications of using a hypothetical science project as the "warm-up" or prompting scenario. Would observed patterns of preferred workmates have been different if I had asked about a social studies project or a creative writing assignment? This is an interesting theoretical and empirical question.

Students were asked to name partners with whom they would enjoy working and with whom they would do a good job. On one hand, in a given classroom, one set of students might be recognized as the most skilled and desirable writers or social studies partners while a somewhat different set would be considered the most desirable science partners; a science project, a social studies project, and a writing assignment each draw upon unique skills and may pique greater or less interest in different students. On the other hand, the body of research on expectations of competence and unidimensional perceptions of ability summarized in Chapter 2 suggests that in many classrooms a single underlying dimension of perceived ability exists (Cohen & Lotan, 1997; Rosenholtz, 1985; Rosenholtz & Simpson, 1984;

Tammivaara, 1982). These findings suggest that the LaCrosse students' responses about preferred workmates might not have been affected much if a different hypothetical prompt had been used.

Adding more uncertainty to the situation is the fact that some of the LaCrosse classrooms seemed to match fairly closely Rosenholtz and Simpson's (1984) depiction of unidimensional classrooms, whereas others had more characteristics of multidimensional classrooms—a distinction to be established and stressed in the coming chapters. As such, one can speculate that the use of a different hypothetical prompt would have been most likely to elicit somewhat different patterns of student preferences in multidimensional classrooms, where students are led to see multiple competencies and interests in their classmates. In contrast, the use of a different prompt might have made little difference in the unidimensional classrooms.

These are indeed interesting aspects to the question concerning different prompts and deserve future research attention. The practicalities of the present study, however, required me to choose a single prompt in asking about preferred workmates; it did not seem feasible to probe for the subtleties associated with multiple prompts. Given these constraints, I invited students to describe any project that interested them, as long as it involved science and was educational. My intention was to help them summon vivid mental images that were inherently interesting to them in order to make the hypothetical question on my survey more concrete and engaging.

CONCLUSION

The combination of qualitative and quantitative data described in this chapter allows for multiple windows upon the dynamics of the 10 classrooms. Moreover, the information gained from any given data source will be used throughout the book to aid in the interpretation of information from other sources. The set of 10 classrooms, situated within five different schools, provides rich variation in context and organization. The next chapter provides a further examination of that variation.

4

Stepping Inside
Ten Classrooms

In the last chapter, the five schools of the study were introduced. Each school experienced a unique set of changes in the wake of the desegregation plan. Now, in this chapter, the particular composition, setting, and dynamics of each classroom are considered. What was the mix of high- and low-SES students in each class? What was the mix of White, Hmong, and other groups? How many students had newly moved to their current schools with the implementation of the busing plan? What leadership styles and decisions distinguished the 10 teachers from one another? What organizational features differentiated the 10 classrooms from one another?

At New Forest Elementary School, I visited Mrs. Nash's and Mrs. Nicholson's classrooms. At Campus Edge, I visited Mr. Clark's and Mrs. Cavanaugh's classes. Mrs. Farr's and Mrs. Fredenburg's classrooms were visited at Fawndale, Mr. Mayes's and Mrs. McCartney's classrooms at Maple Grove, and Mrs. Rolf's and Mr. Rettinger's classrooms at Riverside. These names and all names of students, teachers, administrators, and schools throughout the book are pseudonyms. Only the name LaCrosse is presented unchanged.

Table 4.1 shows the Spring 1994 enrollments of each of these 10 classrooms by race/ethnicity, socioeconomic status (SES), and gender. These class sizes, between 17 and 25, are significantly smaller than elementary class sizes found in some other school districts, especially some urban districts. These enrollments, however, seemed to be the standard for LaCrosse's elementary schools. Table 4.2 shows Spring 1994 enrollments by the school attended in 1991–92, which was the year before the desegregation plan took effect. These tables (together with Table 4.3, discussed at the end of this chapter) can serve as references as I discuss the students, teachers, and events of each classroom in the coming pages and chapters.

Table 4.1. Spring 1994 enrollments of ten classrooms by race/ethnicity, socioeconomic status, and gender

School[a]	Teacher	Categorization by Race/Ethnicity, SES, and Gender								TOTAL
		Non-Asian, Low SES, Male	Non-Asian, Low SES, Female	Non-Asian, High SES, Male	Non-Asian, High SES, Female	Asian, Low SES, Male	Asian, Low SES, Female	Asian, High SES, Male	Asian, High SES, Female	
NF	Nash	3	2	1	5	6	2	0	0	19
NF	Nicholson	1	1	5	6	3	3	0	0	19
CE	Clark	1	0	8	4	2	3	0	0	18
CE	Cavanaugh	4	0	5	4	4	0	0	0	17
FD	Farr	4	1	6	8	2	2	0	0	23
FD	Fredenburg	5	3	5	3	3	4	0	0	23
MG	Mayes	2	1	8	12	2	0	0	0	25
MG	McCartney	2	6	9	6	0	0	0	1	24
RS	Rolf	1	5	7	8	2	0	0	0	23
RS	Rettinger	1	2	8	5	3	3	0	0	22

[a]*School Codes:* NF=New Forest; CE=Campus Edge; FD=Fawndale; MG=Maple Grove; RS=Riverside

Table 4.2. Spring 1994 enrollments of ten classrooms by school attended in 1991–1992

School	Teacher	School Attended in 1991–1992[a]										
		CE	FD	MG	RS	UU	VV	WW	XX	YY	ZZ	TOTAL
New Forest	Nash	3	9	0	0	1	1	0	1	1	3	19
New Forest	Nicholson	5	7	0	0	0	0	4	0	1	2	19
Campus Edge	Clark	11	0	0	0	0	2	0	1	1	3	18
Campus Edge	Cavanaugh	8	1	0	0	1	3	0	0	0	4	17
Fawndale	Farr	4	9	0	0	2	1	4	2	0	1	23
Fawndale	Fredenburg	5	10	0	0	3	1	0	1	0	3	23
Maple Grove	Mayes	0	0	15	0	0	2	0	5	0	3	25
Maple Grove	McCartney	1	0	12	0	1	2	0	4	0	4	24
Riverside	Rolf	0	1	0	15	2	1	0	0	0	4	23
Riverside	Rettinger	0	3	0	10	1	2	0	2	0	4	22

[a] *School Codes:* CE=Campus Edge; FD=Fawndale; MG=Maple Grove; RS=Riverside; UU=non-study school #1; VV=non-study school #2; WW=non-study school #3; XX=non-study school #4; YY=non-study school #5; ZZ=outside of LaCrosse school district

36

DESCRIPTIVE FRAMEWORK FOR ACTIVITY
AND REWARD STRUCTURE

More difficult to document than the demographic composition of each classroom was the activity and reward structure of each. After completing my visits to the 10 classrooms, I attempted to discern from my notes and interviews the teaching styles, decisions, and organizational features that differentiated the 10 settings from one another and that could be expected to affect social relations among students. Early in my fieldwork, I wondered whether a fairly simple continuum from universalism to particularism would wield some power for describing and differentiating the 10 settings. As it was defined in Chapter 2, universalism refers to a situation in which all students are held to the same standards and are treated alike in response to given actions or behaviors. Particularism refers to a situation in which standards, expectations, and treatment of individuals vary student by student, partially in response to students' ascriptive characteristics or backgrounds. Although I began with this continuum as a working guide, as I reviewed the information gathered from each classroom and considered work by other researchers, it proved superficial and insufficient to use this single dimension. None of the teachers was universalistic at all times and in all respects. Similarly, none was purely particularistic. Increasingly, my attention turned to other aspects of task and reward structures.

In reviewing my notes and interviews, I was struck by three frequently appearing themes. The first theme involved the degree to which the students' and the teacher's home lives and past experiences were incorporated into conversations and lessons during the school day. In some of the classrooms, it was common for students to bring photographs, favorite toys, pets, or other things from home to show the class. In some of these same classes, students were often encouraged to share stories or experiences from their home lives during lessons. For example, during a social studies lesson in Mrs. Nash's class, students were looking at a picture of immigrant children in the nineteenth century sitting in church with the boys on one side of the aisle and the girls on the other. Carrie, a Hmong girl, commented that at her church people sat that way, too. Mrs. Nash was encouraging as other students talked about their churches. A lively discussion ensued, with the students agreeing that "it must have been boring to go to church and school in the old days when you had to just sit and listen" for many hours. A kid would probably fall asleep, someone said. Someone else agreed, but said that the church leaders had things with which to "bonk" you on the head if you did fall asleep.

Just as students were likely to share personal stories and experiences in some of the classes, some of the teachers also were likely to do so. It is useful, however, to distinguish between the teacher's personalism and the students' personalism because they were noticeably different in their prevalence in a couple of classrooms. For example, Mrs. Fredenburg incorporated stories of her summer travels into social studies lessons several times during my observations, but she was one of the teachers who was least likely to encourage students to share their out-of-school stories or experiences. Mrs. McCartney, in contrast, shared little about her out-of-school life with the class during the time I was in her classroom, but several times she encouraged students to draw upon their home lives during lessons.

The extent to which students' and teacher's home lives and personal experiences were incorporated into lessons and conversations relates directly to the concept of acquaintance potential, which was discussed in Chapter 2. It also connects with Schofield's (1982/1989) discussion of the transition from relating to classmates as members of in-groups or out-groups to relating to them as individuals with unique interests, abilities, and personality traits. Both theory and prior research suggest that encouraging students to see one another as individuals is an important element of improving intergroup relations.

It is quite apparent that inviting students to share their personal histories or home lives increases acquaintance potential. My classroom observations also suggested to me that a teacher's sharing of personal experiences contributed to an environment in which students were encouraged to consider the ways in which individuals were unique and interesting and the ways in which drawing upon people's backgrounds could make the learning process richer for all. Of course, if a teacher attempts to draw personal experiences and cultural capital into the classroom, it matters whether all members of the class are encouraged to share and contribute, or whether the experiences and capital of some are featured and celebrated to the exclusion of others. I will have more to say about this point later in this chapter and in the book's final chapter.

A second important theme is related to the first, but its breadth or narrowness did not always mirror the levels of teacher and student personalism in the 10 classrooms. This second theme involves the range of activities and performance settings that students encountered in the classroom; that is, the classrooms differed in the extent to which the nature of academic activities varied, either within a single school day or over the course of several days or weeks. In some classrooms, very different types of academic performance and participation were called upon and rewarded from one day to the next, and a wide range of skills was called upon and rewarded in the course of any given week. Later in this chapter, I will describe how Mr. Rettinger structured mathematics instruction to include individual desk work, group collaboration, and a very public game of Around the World during a 2-day period. This variety reflected his emphasis on presenting students with a wide range of performance settings. In contrast, in a classroom like Mr. Mayes's, activities and performance settings were very similar and predictable from one day to the next.

Documenting the range of featured activities and performance settings is a part of determining whether a classroom approached Rosenholtz and Simpson's (1984) description of a multidimensional classroom or came closer to their ideal type of a unidimensional classroom. The breadth or narrowness of a classroom's activities and performance settings, in conjunction with grouping patterns and evaluation practices, can be expected to affect visibility and students' perceptions of their own academic and social standing relative to others in the class (Marshall & Weinstein, 1984; Rosenholtz & Rosenholtz, 1981; Simpson, 1981).

It is important to note, however, that even if a classroom approached the ideal of multidimensionality, this does not guarantee that students were exposed to a multiple-ability orientation of the sort Cohen and Lotan (1995, 1997) have described. For a classroom that featured a wide range of activities and performance settings, it will also be important to note whether the teacher made explicit efforts to impress upon students the fact that different students might bring different dimensions of intellectual ability to tasks, and that each of these dimensions was relevant and valued.

The third theme that appeared frequently in my observational notes involved the degree to which, and frequency with which, the teacher communicated to students the message that all were expected to meet the same standards for academic achievement and behavior. A teacher could communicate the message that all were expected to meet the same standards in a variety of ways. An explicit example appears later in this chapter in the description of Mr. Mayes exhorting a student with, "What are you doing? What are you supposed to be doing? Look around you. What are other people doing?" Mrs. Farr communicated, at least implicitly, that students could gauge their progress relative to others when she took "status of the class," having each student report aloud how many pages of independent reading he or she had completed in the past week.

Communicating that all students were expected to meet the same standards is, of course, a form of universalism. As the summary of Bossert's (1979) study in Chapter 2 stressed, certain task structures create a need or tendency for universalism more than others do. Specifically, classrooms focused on whole-class instruction and other activities in which performance is highly public and comparable among students create this need or tendency. This is partly because, before the observant eyes of an entire class, a teacher seeks to avoid any student suspicions that he or she plays favorites or gives some students special treatment—especially in the realm of behavior and discipline.

In characterizing the 10 classrooms, I keep academic and behavioral expectations separate from each another. While most teachers seemed to treat the two realms similarly, there were at least two exceptions. Mrs. Rolf clearly implied to her students that different students would work at different paces and complete different amounts of work; that was her expectation and her message to students in the academic realm. In the behavioral realm, however, she came closer to expecting all students to conform to the same standards. Mrs. Fredenburg, also, seemed to expect more uniform compliance to high behavioral standards than to academic standards.

Descriptors

The three themes discussed above became the bases for my categorizations of the teachers and classrooms. The first theme suggested the two measures of teacher personalism and student personalism. By teacher personalism, I mean a tendency for the teacher to share personal experiences from outside of the classroom with students. By student personalism, I mean a tendency for students to share personal experiences from outside the classroom, often in response to prompting and encouragement from the teacher.

I must acknowledge that during my time in the classrooms, I tended to view personalism as extending to all students equally. That is, I formed an impression—somewhere between a conscious one and a subconscious one—that, in all of the classrooms that I was coming to think of as personalistic, the teachers did an admirable job of drawing all students' experiences into activities and discussions. I did not note instances in which the teacher made a strong connection with the experiences or home lives of one subset of students to the exclusion of another subset, thereby discouraging the latter group from feelings of belonging and participation. However, in retrospect, I have wondered whether some of the classrooms did draw certain students into activities personalistically more successfully than they drew others. During the writing of this book, I found it impossible to document such patterns with confidence. I simply raise the issue at this point and will return to it in the book's concluding chapter.

The second theme could be captured fairly well by a single measure of the range of performance settings. In the remainder of this chapter and in subsequent chapters, I will lump teacher personalism, student personalism, and the range of performance settings together when I want to describe, roughly and loosely, the overall range of featured and rewarded topics and settings in each classroom.

The third theme, again, seemed to require two measures: (1) rigor and uniformity of academic standards and (2) rigor and uniformity of disciplinary standards. Although it is not necessary that uniform expectations go hand in hand with high expectations, that was the situation in these 10 classrooms. That is, if a teacher communicated to students that all were expected to meet the same expectations, those expectations tended to be quite rigorous.

In rating each classroom on each of the five measures, I relied on my observational notes and interviews. For teacher personalism and student personalism, I tallied each occurrence of stories or experiences from outside the classroom entering informal discussions or formal lessons. In assessing the range of performance settings, I noted how varied the learning environments were within single days and over the span of all the days on which I observed the particular classroom. Variation in task structure was considered. Possible task structures included individual desk work, small-group work, whole-class instruction, individual students making presentations or leading the class in a lesson, and lessons that took place outside the classroom. Also, variation in learning materials was considered. For example, if students worked in small groups most days for mathematics lessons, but the work involved solving problems from the textbook on one day, learning to use calculators on another, and using Cuisenaire rods on another, this was considered evidence of a wide range of performance settings.

In assessing the rigor and uniformity of academic and disciplinary standards, a teacher's comments to individual students or to the entire class were noted, as were the teacher's comments in the interview. Some teachers made statements that revealed a tendency toward high and uniform standards, while others made statements which revealed standards that varied student by student. Both types of statements were considered in rating teachers.

At the end of this chapter, I will explicitly classify each of the 10 classrooms according to the five dimensions of activity and reward structure just discussed. First, though, I offer some vignettes, quotations, and other qualitative accounts as I introduce the 10 classrooms in an order that follows quite directly from the conceptual framework I have been describing.

THE TEN CLASSROOMS

Mr. Rettinger's Class

Mr. Rettinger's class was one of the two classes I visited at Riverside Elementary School. I offer this classroom as the one in the study that had the widest range of featured and rewarded topics and settings. The class-room was very striking because of the wide variety of learning activities students encountered in the course of a day or a week. There was a high degree of continuity between one day's lessons and the next day's lessons, and even between one day's science lesson and the next day's math les-son. But this continuity in the lessons' substance and subject matters was coupled with great variation in the nature of the activities and performance settings. Indeed, Rettinger's class approached the ideal of the multidimen-sional classroom as nearly as any classroom in the study.

Some of the activities were quite traditional; these activities, such as students individually working through math exercises from a textbook or several students being called to the front of the room to solve problems on the chalkboard as the rest of the class watched, take place in the majority of elementary school classrooms almost every day. Some of the other ac-tivities featured in Rettinger's class, however, were less traditional and often took advantage of Riverside's setting in the midst of nature.

For example, during the winter, the class was studying units of mea-surement in science. Capitalizing upon the previous days' snowstorm, Mr. Rettinger instructed students to don their jackets and boots, grab meter sticks, and follow him outside to measure the snow depth at various loca-tions. The students worked very well in groups of two or three to measure in drifts, beneath trees, and in windswept clearings. On another occasion, in the spring, the class walked about a quarter of a mile to what was called the "frog pond." Notebooks in hand, they had been instructed to write the names of as many types of flora and fauna as they could identify. Still an-other encounter with nature as a learning aid came when Mr. Rettinger posted a chart at the front of the classroom on which the class tallied the number of eagles students had seen around their homes and the school each week. Through this exercise, the class learned about data collection and graphing.

Finally, yet another innovative and successful science lesson was dur-ing the class's study of flight. Over the course of several days, each stu-dent constructed several paper airplanes. With desks moved aside and a calibrated strip of tape down the center of the classroom, students lofted their planes to see how far each would fly. With one day's most and least successful flights in mind, students spent the next day's science period adapting their planes, altering the size or shape of their previous designs. By the 2nd day of plane building, some planes were flying far enough that the class had to move to the school's gymnasium for their final trials.

Providing an example of the noteworthy continuity of substance that characterized Rettinger's classroom in conjunction with the varied activities, the students entered the room the morning after their airplane flights to find instructions on the chalkboard telling them that, in order to begin the morning's math lessons, they should calculate the range and average of the previous day's flight distances.

A main point I wish to make (and which will be reiterated in Chapter 5) is that the wide range of activities and performance settings allowed a large number of students to excel and receive praise over the course of a given day or a given week. Sometimes the outcomes were surprising to me.

Over the course of 2 days in the spring, I had noted in my observational log that the students had encountered several quite different types of math activities. Halfway through the 2nd day's math period, Mr. Rettinger said that they would play a game of Around the World. To play Around the World one student would begin by getting out of his chair and standing behind the chair of the student next to him. Mr. Rettinger would hold up a math flash card and the two students would try to give the correct answer to the card's problem. If the standing student was not the first to answer correctly, he would take the other's seat and the other student would move to stand behind the next person's seat. The object of the game was to answer enough questions quickly and correctly to move all the way around the room and back to one's own seat. As this game began, I wrote in my notes that it was a very public display of ability.

Soon a boy named Jerry answered a question correctly from his chair and became the one to stand and to try to move around the room. Jerry was not very well accepted by the other students. Although Jerry was quite smart, he was a restless and nervous student. He was often withdrawn from lessons. But in this situation he did very well, answering questions before some opponents who were regarded as the best math students in the class. Jerry did, in fact, win the game and receive compliments from Mr. Rettinger and a lot of the other students. I wrote in my notes that, in a class with a wide range of abilities, it was somewhat risky for Mr. Rettinger to initiate this game of Around the World because there could be some glaring mismatches as students competed with one another. But, in light of Jerry's somewhat surprising victory, the game seemed to have served the purpose of challenging some assumptions about who the "best" math students were.

I would not use this anecdote about Around the World to argue against all of the research that has shown the benefits of cooperation as opposed to competition for improving intergroup relations (e.g., Cohen & Lotan, 1997; Metz, 1986/1992; Schofield, 1982/1989; Slavin, 1980). But the anecdote does suggest that a certain level of visibility and public performance can serve to challenge any simple conception of a unidimensional status hierarchy *if* it is accompanied by a wide range of featured and rewarded activities and competencies. Indeed, I am not making the argument that visibility was low in Rettinger's class and that, therefore, a rigid and agreed-upon hierarchy of perceived ability was avoided among his students. Rather, I am arguing that because of the classroom's wide range of activities, different students were able to excel on different days. The fact that some activities were very public in nature actually contributed to the challenging of potential assumptions about a single and fixed dimension of academic ability and status.

Rettinger's class was also noteworthy for its high degree of personalism. Students periodically brought pictures or favorite possessions for show-and-tell. This sharing provided the group insights into one another's home lives. Mr. Rettinger sometimes shared stories of what was happening at his home and, in fact, his personal stories sometimes were incorporated into lessons. During a unit on poetry, the class was having a discussion about the ways authors get ideas. During the discussion, Mr. Rettinger told about a short story he had written called "Halloween Heroes." He described in detail how he had gotten his ideas, how he had sat down at home with pencil and paper, and how he had gone about writing the story. This level of personalism was typical in Rettinger's classroom, but contrasted sharply with some of the other classrooms I visited.

Who were the students in Rettinger's class? At the time of my spring visit, there were 22 students in the class. As Table 4.1 shows, 6 of these students were low-SES Asian Americans. Another 3 were low-SES White students. The remaining 13 were high-SES White students.

This spring enrollment of 22 was reduced from the 32 students who had been in Rettinger's class at the start of the school year. Due to the overcrowding in the classrooms of both Mr. Rettinger and Mrs. Rolf, the district approved the hiring of a third teacher for Riverside's fourth grade about 2 months into the school year. This allowed for an important reduction in class size for both Mr. Rettinger and Mrs. Rolf.

Eighteen of the 22 spring students had been in the LaCrosse school district 2 years earlier, distributed among five schools (see Table 4.2). It is important to consider whether or not students had changed schools in the wake of the desegregation plan. For those who had, it is important to consider whether they entered their new schools with large numbers of their former schoolmates or in relative isolation. As Table 4.2 shows, 10 of Rettinger's students had attended Riverside in 1991–92. These 10 included 1 low-SES White student and 9 high-SES White students. Of the other 8 students who had been in the district in 1991–92, 3 had attended Fawndale Elementary School together before the busing plan; these 3 were all low-SES Asian Americans. Everyone else was either the sole student from his or her 1991–92 school or was accompanied by one former schoolmate.

Mrs. Nash's Class

Next I will describe Mrs. Nash's class at New Forest Elementary School, one of the classes that were just below Rettinger's on the continuum of featured and rewarded topics and settings. My initial visit to Nash's classroom was on the first day of the 1993–94 school year. The classroom was bright and inviting. New Forest's building was only one year old and the classroom's attractive carpet, cabinets, sink, desks, and chairs caught my attention immediately.

As the students arrived for their first day of fourth grade, Mrs. Nash greeted them as they entered the room in pairs, in trios, or one by one. They were asked to draw one card apiece from a deck of playing cards, which were face down on a counter at the side of the classroom. Each student's playing card matched a card on one of the desks. The desk with the matching card was where Mrs. Nash wanted the student to sit for the first part of the school year. The desks were arranged in clusters of three or four. Mrs. Nash's intention was that the use of the playing cards would lead students to meet new people, would avoid a situation in which students sat only with their old friends, and would mix the students randomly with respect to gender, race, and neighborhood. Although Mrs. Nash probably would not have used the term, this effort with the playing cards was an attempt to formally encourage acquaintance potential among students who may not have known one another previously.

I was eager to observe how the students would greet one another and interact in their first moments as fourth-grade classmates. The finding of desks provided some interesting insights into both the students' preferences and Mrs. Nash's leadership style. A Hmong girl, Carrie, was among the first students to arrive. She drew a playing card and took the seat with the matching card as Mrs. Nash had intended. Soon afterward two Hmong boys, Kong and Neng, entered the room and, before Mrs. Nash had a chance to explain to them about the playing cards, they took the two remaining seats at Carrie's desk cluster. The three students spoke to each other in Hmong and Carrie pointed toward the counter with the playing cards. The two boys shrugged and remained in the seats they had chosen next to Carrie.

Most of the other students drew playing cards as Mrs. Nash had intended, although a few others may have missed the instructions or ignored them in order to sit by friends. A few students arrived late from their buses, and Mrs. Nash directed them to desks that remained open. It is not clear to me whether Mrs. Nash had noticed immediately that Kong and Neng did not draw cards, but rather chose seats with Carrie. I think she probably noticed fairly quickly that these three Hmong students had ended up sitting together and that this arrangement was somewhat contrary to her plans for randomly mixing the seating.

The pattern that was displayed in the sequence described above is one that I observed several times during my visits to this classroom throughout the year: Mrs. Nash structured classroom activities with the intention of mixing the students in new and different groupings, but she was unlikely to be rigid about following her plans if it appeared that some students were uncomfortable with the situation or if it would be disruptive to the flow of classroom activities to enforce her plans rigidly.

Mrs. Nash's academic and behavioral expectations, as compared with those of the other nine teachers in the study, were fairly lax. Nash's class seemed to move through the mathematics curriculum, which was based upon a textbook and worksheets used in all of the district's fourth-grade classrooms, at a slower pace than most of the other classes. It was very rare for Mrs. Nash to assign homework in any subject. Students were expected to read at home and practice with math flash cards, but these were not things that were checked upon or assessed regularly in class. Regarding behavior, Mrs. Nash allowed more off-task talking and moving around the classroom than did most of the other teachers.

I will argue in the next chapter that the rigor of academic and behavioral expectations, along with the degree to which a teacher varied her or his demands and expectations student by student, seemed to influence which students were eager and able to participate. Rigor and uniformity of expectations also influenced which students were praised in a visible fashion, which students answered wrongly in a visible fashion, and which students were scolded in a visible fashion.

At the time of my spring visit, there were 19 students in Nash's class. Of these students 8 were low-SES Asian Americans, 5 were low-SES White students, and 6 were high-SES White students.

Sixteen of the 19 students had been in the school district 2 years earlier, distributed among six different schools. Of course, none of the students had attended New Forest in 1991–92 because it had not yet opened. As Table 4.2 shows, the largest group of students in Nash's class who had attended the same school in 1991–92 were 9 students who had attended Fawndale Elementary School. These 9 included 5 Hmong students, 2 low-SES White students, and 2 high-SES White students. Each of the other students in Nash's class was either the sole student from his or her 1991–92 school or was accompanied by just a couple of former schoolmates.

Mrs. Nicholson's Class

Mrs. Nicholson's classroom was next door to Mrs. Nash's at New Forest. In comparison to Nash's class, Nicholson's class had a larger representation of high-SES students. Also, Nicholson's students were more likely to be among former schoolmates. At the time of my spring visit, there were 19 students in Nicholson's class. Of these students, 6 were low-SES Asian Americans, 2 were low-SES White students, and 11 were high-SES White students.

Seventeen of the 19 students in Nicholson's class had attended LaCrosse public schools 2 years earlier, distributed among four schools. Of these 17 students, 7 had attended Fawndale together in 1991–92, including all 6 of the Asian American students and 1 high-SES White student. Five other high-SES White students had attended Campus Edge together in 1991–92. Four other high-SES White students had attended yet another of the district's schools together in that year. The remaining student who had been in the district in 1991–92, a low-SES White girl, was the sole representative of her former school.

Regarding the larger representation (11) of high-SES White students in Nicholson's class, a perceptive reader of my classroom descriptions mentioned to me that influential or active parents may have lobbied for their children's enrollment with Mrs. Nicholson. The fact that 4 of these students were from one school and another 5 were from Campus Edge, a school known for parental involvement, supports this suggestion. While I have no firsthand knowledge of any such lobbying, I agree that it is likely that it took place.

During my first days with Nicholson's class, my strongest impressions were of the seriousness and intensity with which she led the students through their academic work. Mrs. Nicholson was, at once, a warm, nurturing person and a teacher with high expectations for her students. With mathematics, in particular, instructional time was a very focused and fairly fast paced part of the school day. Likely as a result of the seriousness and fast pace of the lessons, many students were reluctant to raise their hands to volunteer answers.

Mrs. Nicholson's teaching style included some practices that may have discouraged or alienated students of lower ability. In contrast, however, Mrs. Nicholson also made some explicit efforts to draw students of lower ability into discussions and lessons. An example of a practice that discouraged or alienated some students involved the arrangement of desks and Mrs. Nicholson's use of the overhead projector. The desks were arranged in clusters of three or four. At the beginning of the year, students had been allowed to select their own seats. In choosing these seats, it happened that three of the six desk clusters were occupied by high-SES students almost exclusively; 10 of the 11 students at these desk clusters were high-SES. The other three desk clusters were occupied by low-SES students almost exclusively; 8 of the 9 students at these clusters were low-SES.

Mrs. Nicholson often stood at the overhead projector during mathematics lessons, writing on transparencies and speaking to the class. Because she was right-handed, she stood on the left side of the projector as she wrote and taught. This meant that her back often was turned partially or fully to two of the three desk clusters that were occupied primarily by low-SES students. Most of her questions, at the times she was using the overhead projector, were directed to the three desk clusters that were occupied primarily by high-SES students. During these times, many of the students at the other three clusters tended to daydream or to talk to one another quietly.

This tendency to focus her attention on the high-SES students was limited to certain parts of the school day, however, and was most noticeable to me at the beginning of the school year. On the same days that I noted Mrs. Nicholson's style at the overhead projector, there were also times when she would ask one of the daydreaming students a direct question about the lesson. In doing this, she tended to use a soft, patient voice and to ask a relatively easy question. These efforts were quite effective in drawing daydreaming students into the lesson.

One of the students who was most likely to daydream in the fall was Jim, a low-SES White boy. Jim's home life was very troubled, and he received medication for an attention deficit disorder. He was among those whose attention would drift when Mrs. Nicholson's back was turned to him. At the time of my winter visit, however, Mrs. Nicholson had seated Jim at a more central position in the classroom, and she made efforts to call upon him and maintain his attention.

Toward the end of one day in January, Mrs. Nicholson asked Jim to teach the class a dice game called Five Thousand. He explained that it was something he had learned from a relative, who played the game at a local bar. After Jim taught the game to the class, they broke into groups of four or five and played the game for about 20 minutes. Mrs. Nicholson stressed to the class that they should think about how this game called upon their arithmetic skills.

A couple of things struck me about the teaching of this dice game. First, it was a time for Jim to be central to the class, as he shared something of interest and value. Jim was tentative and nervous as he began to explain the game, but gradually gained confidence. He seemed to enjoy the experience and to care genuinely that his classmates learn the game correctly. Second, it took some thought and effort by Mrs. Nicholson to turn a barroom game into something that would be presented to the students primarily as being relevant to sharpening their computation skills. The skills and experiences Jim could share from his home were not things that would be recognized or rewarded in a lot of classrooms. It was clear that Mrs. Nicholson wanted this to be a source of pride and satisfaction to Jim, as well as a source of learning for the class.

Along with my observations of this class, my conversations with Mrs. Nicholson made clear the difficult decisions a teacher faces in teaching a very heterogeneous classroom. When I asked Mrs. Nicholson whether she had made conscious changes in her teaching style in the 2 years since the beginning of the desegregation plan, she said that she had had to give a lot of thought to the high-ability students, a lot of thought to "how to challenge them and keep them going." Before coming to New Forest, Mrs. Nicholson had taught fairly disadvantaged students at Fawndale. While she was supportive of the desegregation plan and enjoyed her heterogeneous classes at New Forest, she found the situation challenging. Her heavy attention paid to the high-SES and high-achieving students early in the year quite likely resulted from her desire to challenge those students. Her relatively easy questions directed to other students and her strategies with a student like Jim resulted from her desire to maintain the interest and involvement of lower achieving students.

In light of these various occurrences from Mrs. Nicholson's class, I contend that she achieved what might be called partial success in assigning competence to low-status students, as this strategy has been described by Cohen and Lotan (1997). When she allocated time for Jim to teach the dice game to the class and made a point of stressing the value the game had to the class's learning of mathematics, she directed public praise in a very genuine way to a skill that a low-SES and low-achieving student possessed. On the other hand, when she asked relatively easy questions of disengaged students in a soft voice, she was not establishing a situation in which correct answers from these students would be recognized as academic accomplishments worthy of much admiration by classmates.

How each teacher responded to a heterogeneous classroom, how varied were each teacher's academic and behavioral expectations, and how wide was each classroom's range of featured and rewarded tasks and activities are central to a consideration of social relations among the students. Each of these issues has implications for which students become defined as desirable workmates or playmates. Each of these issues also has implications for how a student perceives his or her own role and worth within the classroom.

Mr. Clark's Class

Joining Nash's and Nicholson's classes at roughly the same point on the continuum of featured and rewarded topics and settings were Mr. Clark's and Mrs. Cavanaugh's classes at Campus Edge Elementary School. I will describe Clark's class first. Most mornings began with a discussion of current events. Mr. Clark would prompt the class with questions about news items that the students might have seen in a newspaper or on television or might have heard about from their parents. The topics ranged from issues that affected the school or the city, to state, national, or international news. The tone of the discussions was always relaxed. Sometimes Mr. Clark would devise a game to engage the class. One morning in January, three items were written on the board: "Welcome back, _ _. _ _ _ _ _"; " _ _ _ _ _ _ _"; and " _ _ _ _ _ _ _ _."

Students took turns guessing letters, as one would for games like Hangman or Wheel of Fortune. The answers were MR. PLANK, POVERTY, and STRANDED. The first puzzle was simply to welcome me back to the classroom. The second puzzle prompted a discussion about a front-page article in that morning's local paper about the high poverty rate among Asian American youth in Wisconsin. The third puzzle led to a discussion about a young man who had become stranded while climbing on a dangerous part of the rocky bluffs that border LaCrosse to the east (and which were visible from the classroom's windows).

The discussion of current events usually lasted for 10–15 minutes. On some days, additional time was allocated for the students and Mr. Clark to tell the class about things they had seen or done outside of school. Mr. Clark had certain goals in mind as he began a school day with these discussions of current events and personal experiences. First, it was an activity that had a relatively serious tone (which announced that "class was now in session") but still remained uninhibiting enough to help students ease into the school day. It was apparent in each of the 10 classrooms that some students found it difficult to be alert and attentive at the beginning of a school day, while other students were ready to concentrate and work from the moment they entered the classroom. The serious but relaxed discussions in Clark's class were effective in gaining the interest and attention of most students.

Interestingly, during one of my visits to New Forest Elementary School, Mrs. Nicholson had told me that one of the things that had become apparent to her earlier in her teaching career was that students from disadvantaged homes often needed 15–20 minutes at the beginning of the school day to talk about themselves and to get ready to learn. Without this time, she said, the students' attention would be lost for the rest of the day. Mr. Clark had taught at New Forest during the 1992–93 school year and worked closely with Mrs. Nicholson. It is possible that they had discussed the importance of beginning the school day with activities that were calming and welcoming.

Mr. Clark also accomplished a second goal through the discussions of current events. He placed a great deal of emphasis on making students aware of the world around them. He often assigned homework projects that required students to collaborate with their parents in gathering information from newspapers or magazines, and he had various newspapers available for students to take if they did not have access to newspapers at home. At other times, students were asked to gather information about their family histories. These assignments reflected a focus that extended beyond the walls of the classroom. Although all of the teachers in the study drew upon some topics and events from beyond the walls of the classroom, Mr. Clark was one who was especially noteworthy in this respect.

At the time of my spring visit, there were 18 students in the class. Of these students 5 were low-SES Asian Americans, and another was a low-SES White student. The remaining 12 were high-SES White students.

Fifteen of the 18 students had been in the school district 2 years earlier, distributed among four schools. The majority of the high-SES students in Clark's class (9 of 12) had been at Campus Edge in 1991–92. Additionally, 2 of the Asian American students had been at Campus Edge at that time. Each of the other students was either the sole representative of his or her 1991–92 school or was accompanied by one former schoolmate.

Mrs. Cavanaugh's Class

In comparison with Mr. Clark's class, Mrs. Cavanaugh's class had a smaller group of high-SES students who had attended Campus Edge prior to the desegregation plan. Also, Cavanaugh's class differed from Clark's in that her class had a larger representation of low-SES White students. At the time of my spring visit, Cavanaugh's class had 17 students, of whom 4 were low-SES Asian Americans, another 4 were low-SES White students, and 9 were high-SES White students.

Thirteen of the 17 had attended LaCrosse public schools 2 years earlier, distributed among four schools. Eight had attended Campus Edge in 1991–92, including 1 Asian American student, 1 low-SES White student, and 6 high-SES White students. Of the other students, 2 Asian American students and a low-SES White student had attended another of the district's schools together in 1991–92. The remaining 2 students who had been in the district in 1991–92 were the sole representatives of their former schools.

Of the 10 classrooms in the study, Cavanaugh's was one of those most affected by students moving in and out of the school during the year. At the time of my fall visit, there were 19 students in the classroom. During the school year, five of these students left Campus Edge while three new students arrived to finish the year in Cavanaugh's class. Additionally, two other students arrived part of the way into the school year and stayed relatively short periods of time, moving before the end of the year.

The changes in attendance zones that were imposed by the desegregation plan were a part of the reason that Mrs. Cavanaugh was encountering a higher level of student mobility than she had experienced in previous years. She now had a higher number of students whose families rented their homes or apartments than she had experienced in the past. These families tended to move more often than other families did. But, also, she said that student mobility was a factor that varied from year to year; in 1992–93, the first year of the desegregation plan, she had not experienced as many students moving into and out of her classroom.

The high level of student mobility presented Mrs. Cavanaugh with multiple challenges. Regarding academic matters, the arrival of students from different schools or districts augmented the challenges of targeting teaching materials to what was already a heterogeneous group in terms of skills and aptitudes. Moreover, the multiple arrivals and departures of students added to Mrs. Cavanaugh's challenges in building cohesion among the students and in establishing strong teacher-student relationships.

Despite these obstacles, Cavanaugh's class had perhaps the warmest and most supportive relationships among the students of any of the 10 classrooms I visited. Certainly there were some quarrels or antagonistic relationships among students, but it was in Cavanaugh's class that I most often noted my surprise at displays of support and friendship between students from whom I would not have expected such displays.

Analyses in later chapters will show that Cavanaugh's class was especially distinct from the other classrooms in the status or roles of low-SES White students. An anecdote centered around Ed and Bruce, two low-SES White boys in the class, is informative. During my first visit to Cavanaugh's class, in the fall, several students came to Mrs. Cavanaugh after the students' morning break to use the restrooms and told her that "Ed and Bruce were playing Bloody Murder again." I never learned the full details of Bloody Murder, but it involved turning out the bathroom lights and scaring people. Mrs. Cavanaugh spoke to Ed and Bruce sternly, but privately, about this incident.

Later in the day, Mrs. Cavanaugh was calling upon students to stand in front of the class and read aloud stories they had written as a part of their unit on Native American creation stories. Ed was the fourth student to be called upon. He did not want to come forward and said that he could not find his story. While this discussion was occurring, Bruce was looking for his story in his desk, with the help of the boy who sat next to him. This prompted Mrs. Cavanaugh to ask the boy next to Ed to help him find his work.

With what was apparently enthusiasm about the concept of helping, four students eventually helped Ed sort through his papers until he found his story. One of these helpers accompanied Ed to the front of the class, where the two read Ed's story to the class together. Ed's unhappiness and reserve had instantly vanished; with a newfound smile he volunteered to help the next student, Chao, read his story. Chao wanted his friend Ja to help, so Mrs. Cavanaugh suggested that both Ed and Ja accompany Chao to the front of the class. Finally, as the conclusion to this contagious helpfulness, five or six students offered to help Bruce read his story to the class. However, because the class had to leave for their time at the computer lab, Mrs. Cavanaugh said Bruce's story would have to wait for another day.

As the year proceeded, Ed emerged as a popular member of the class. While he occasionally displayed a temper, mischievousness, or lapses in paying attention, he was generally cheerful and eager to work with others. Other students, in turn, enjoyed working and playing with him. Bruce, on the other hand, moved to Fredenburg's class at Fawndale Elementary School which was, by coincidence, one of the other classrooms I was visiting. When I saw him at Fawndale, Bruce was periodically scolded and usually withdrawn. He did not establish many friendships.

It is difficult to guess how Bruce would have fared if he had remained in Cavanaugh's class throughout the year. But in reflecting upon Ed and Bruce, and their interactions with teachers and classmates, I was struck by the influence a teacher and a classroom setting can have upon a student's status among his peers. What Mrs. Cavanaugh had done with Ed and Bruce on the day of Bloody Murder and creation stories, she continued to do for Ed throughout the year; that is, when misbehavior occurred, she reprimanded sternly but without causing embarrassment in front of the class. Her disciplinary style had many of the traits of those used in the multitask classrooms first described by Bossert (1979) and further described by Metz (1986/1992). Mrs. Cavanaugh seemed to seek private moments for most of her disciplinary responses and then to take the time needed to search for the roots of the misbehavior and to deal with a student's feelings.

Further, Mrs. Cavanaugh encouraged all students to contribute to the academic activities of the class. And she established a classroom in which one's peers were not only willing but eager to draw reluctant classmates into these activities.

Mrs. Farr's Class

Characterized by a slightly narrower level of personalism, but still featuring a wide range of performance settings, was Mrs. Farr's classroom at Fawndale Elementary School. Mrs. Farr faced the challenging prospect of teaching a mixed-grade class, comprising both fourth- and fifth-grade students. This fact, coupled with the diversity of backgrounds and abilities present within even a single grade's students at Fawndale, presented a potentially daunting teaching situation. Mrs. Farr, however, was quite skillful at eliciting enthusiasm and effort from almost every student.

For most lessons and activities, the fourth- and fifth-grade students were taught jointly. There were some activities for which the students were split according to grade. Keyboarding was a 6-week unit taught by another teacher and was for fourth graders exclusively. The two grades followed different social studies curricula for the first part of the school year. But for the majority of the school day, all of Farr's students functioned as one class.

Mrs. Farr was very knowledgeable about debates and advances in educational theory and practice. She took the idea of recognizing multiple forms of intelligence and aptitude very seriously. She cited Howard Gardner's writings in one conversation with me. Indeed, I would venture to say she was the one teacher in the study who used techniques that were true to Cohen and Lotan's (1997) description of a multiple-ability treatment. The wide range of activities and performance settings Mrs. Farr presented to her students, as well as her explicit discussion of multiple competencies, reflected her goals and philosophies as a teacher.

In teaching mathematics, she used a variety of resources and tools. Early in the school year, the class learned to use calculators. The set of brand-new calculators they used included one that was specially designed for use on an overhead projector. With this, the whole class could see Mrs. Farr's demonstrations as the calculator's keys and solutions were projected onto the screen before them.

Later in the year, the students used Cuisenaire rods, sets of colored rods of different lengths, for a mathematics unit. With these, the students actually solved simple algebra problems, although Mrs. Farr did not describe the exercises as algebra, per se. An example of the problems the students were solving is this: If one orange rod equals three yellow rods, what part of an orange rod equals one yellow rod? As Mrs. Farr introduced this mathematics unit to the students, she talked to them about the fact that there are many forms of intelligence. Using these rods would draw upon spatial intelligence, which was one of these forms. Some people are especially strong in spatial intelligence, she said, just as other people are strong in other areas of intelligence.

In the next chapter, I give more attention to the effects of presenting students with a wide range of performance and achievement settings. Mrs. Farr was one of the teachers who were most committed to this emphasis in their teaching. A further example of this emphasis is presented by the teaching of the Hmong language in her classroom. She and another teacher had applied for a grant that allowed them to hire a Hmong man from the community to come into their classrooms three times each week to teach students to read, write, and speak Hmong. The students' reactions to the Hmong lessons were interesting. For the four Hmong students in the class, it was a chance to be leaders among their peers. As I observed one day's lesson, these four students seemed more assertive than usual and were consistently among the first to answer the instructor's questions. As I noted this, however, I also noted that these were four students who were enthusiastic and assertive students in general; they were markedly more assertive than most of the Hmong students I observed in other classrooms. When I mentioned my perception to Mrs. Farr, she agreed that this was an activity in which the Hmong students could play lead roles, but she also pointed out that they sometimes struggled with the lessons because they could speak and understand Hmong but were learning to write the language for the first time.

Among the non-Hmong students in the class, there were mixed reactions to the Hmong lessons. Although the lessons appeared to be difficult for almost everyone, most students exhibited at least moderate enthusiasm. A few of the White boys were the exception in that they appeared to truly dislike and resent the lessons. In fact, as one boy walked past me, he said to me that he hated the lessons. My perception—one with which Mrs. Farr agreed—was that, for some students who generally excelled academically and who were classroom leaders, it was threatening to be presented with a task on which other students might be at a distinct advantage.

My observations of Farr's class impressed on me that, as one thinks about the degree of visibility of achievement and behaviors in a classroom, it is important to also consider the range of activities and performance settings. If one thinks of a group's interactions as a series of games, one should ask whether the same game, with the same rules, is being played day after day. Or, alternatively, is there variation in the game, the rules, and the reward structure? How are these things related to the form and stability of status and prestige structures? These are issues to be addressed in the coming chapters.

There were 23 students in Farr's class at the time of my spring visit. Of these students, 4 were low-SES Asian Americans, and 5 were low-SES non-Asian students, 4 White and 1 African American. The remaining 14 were high-SES White students.

Twenty-two of the 23 students had been in the school district 2 years earlier, distributed among six schools. The largest group of students who had attended school together in 1991–92 were 9 students who had attended Fawndale. These 9 included all 4 of the Asian American students, 2 of the low-SES non-Asian students, and 3 of the high-SES students. Further, a group of 4 students had attended Campus Edge together in 1991–92, and another group of 4 students had attended another of the district's schools together. Each of the other 5 students who had been in the district in 1991–92 was either the sole student from his or her former school or was accompanied by one past schoolmate.

Mrs. Rolf's Class

Mrs. Rolf taught at Riverside Elementary School. At the start of the school year, 31 students were enrolled in her class. This was an almost unmanageable number, especially because this number included 4 students with special needs and several others who remained in the classroom all day and exhibited fairly disruptive behavior. Both the physical space of the classroom and Mrs. Rolf's ability to monitor and teach all of the students were strained to their limits. As mentioned earlier in this chapter, because Mr. Rettinger's classroom at Riverside was equally crowded, the district approved the hiring of a third teacher for Riverside's fourth grade about 2 months into the school year. Eleven students from Mrs. Rolf's class and 10 students from Mr. Rettinger's class were moved to the new fourth-grade classroom. These changes made the management of classroom space, instruction, and discipline much easier for the teachers.

A couple of boys, however, continued to be disruptive and were the recipients of a very large proportion of Mrs. Rolf's time and attention. One of these boys, Rob, had been diagnosed with autism. The other boy, Gene, had a very unstable home life and had great difficulty concentrating and controlling his temper. One morning in the spring both boys were absent. Gene arrived at school in the middle of the day. During the afternoon, Mrs. Rolf commented to me about how different, and easily managed, the classroom had been without those two boys. It was true that the whole atmosphere of the class had been different during their absence.

Mrs. Rolf was faced with a group of students with extremely varied abilities and needs. Partly in response to this, she allocated major parts of most school days for students' individual work; during this time they were free to move around the room if they needed reference books or art materials, and to ask questions and confer with other students. Routinely, four or five projects for individual work were provided, often listed on the chalkboard as a reminder to the students. The projects tended to be of varying difficulty and to call for varying degrees of self-direction. Mrs. Rolf told me that her intention was that students with the highest ability levels, or those who worked at the fastest paces, might complete all of the projects. Other students might not get beyond the third project. Mrs. Rolf said she accepted these differences in completion rates and achievement; a student could still get good grades and evaluations if Mrs. Rolf perceived that the student was exerting effort.

Consistent with her varying academic expectations, Mrs. Rolf also seemed to desire that her students avoid academic anxiety. She seemed to be careful in choosing her words when she spoke about tests, grades, and the like. In discussing a language assessment, she said to the class, "Tomorrow you'll quiz yourselves on this." Most other teachers would have said, "Tomorrow I'll test you on this." In collecting math assignments, she tended to say, "I want to take a look at these." Many other teachers would have said, "I'm going to collect these and record your scores."

In many ways, Rolf's classroom resembled the multitask classes described by Bossert (1979) and the multidimensional classes described by Rosenholtz and Simpson (1984). In particular, Rolf's class matched these others in the way students worked on a variety of tasks, at their own paces, with relatively low visibility. Also, Mrs. Rolf stressed student autonomy and downplayed grades and competitiveness.

A final note about Rolf's classroom is that it lacked the outgoing leaders that some of the other classrooms had. Mentioning this fact to me, Mrs. Rolf said that she thought the absence of strong leaders had led to a lack of cohesion and classroom spirit. In classrooms like Mayes's or, to some extent, Farr's, students who were strongest academically tended to be assertive and central to the classroom's social life. In contrast, in Rolf's class, the students who were strongest academically were fairly quiet and did not set the social tone for the classroom as a whole. An interesting question about cause and effect arises, of course, as one can speculate that Mrs. Rolf's very individualized task organization discouraged classroom cohesion and the establishment of student leaders who could or would set a social tone for the entire class.

At the time of my spring visit, there were 23 students in Rolf's class. Two of these were low-SES Asian Americans, 6 were low-SES White students, and the remaining 15 were high-SES White students.

Nineteen of the 23 students had been in the district 2 years earlier, distributed among four schools. Fifteen had attended Riverside in 1991–92, including 2 low-SES White students and 13 high-SES White students. The other 4 students who had been in the district in 1991–92 were either the sole students from their former schools or were accompanied by one past schoolmate.

Mrs. Fredenburg's Class

I have already described Mrs. Farr's class at Fawndale Elementary School. The other class I visited there was Mrs. Fredenburg's. Mrs. Fredenburg was in her last year of teaching when I visited her classroom; she would retire at the end of the school year. During the year, it was necessary for her to be absent fairly often, and for prolonged periods at a few times.

It was my impression that Mrs. Fredenburg never established close relationships with most of her students. I do not know whether this lack of close relationships was a direct result of her many absences or whether it was typical of her classroom dynamics over the years. In any case, in addition to a lack of close relationships, she seemed to gain only partial respect and authority as she related to her students. During my winter visit, she asked one boy to do something, and as he refused, I heard him mutter, "That's okay, she's not the real teacher anyway."

Mrs. Fredenburg was a strict disciplinarian. She wanted her students to remain serious and on-task at most times during the school day. She had a tendency, however, to communicate her disciplinary and academic expectations in a manner that was sarcastic, inconsistent, and ambiguous. Students often seemed confused, unsure of whether she was joking or angry.

It is difficult for me to give a concise characterization of Mrs. Fredenburg's class because the tone and dynamics of her classroom changed a lot from one day to the next. It was not the case that the set of activities and lessons with which students were engaged changed a lot between days. Rather, what changed were things like the level of calm, the degree to which students seemed to understand instructions, and the level of engagement in tasks.

At the time of my spring visit, there were 23 students in Fredenburg's class. Seven were low-SES Asian Americans, 8 were low-SES White students, and the remaining 8 were high-SES White students.

Twenty of the 23 students had been in the school district 2 years earlier, distributed among five schools. Ten of these students had attended Fawndale together in 1991–92, including 4 Asian American students, 5 low-SES White students, and 1 high-SES White student. Further, 5 students had attended Campus Edge Elementary School together in 1991–92, while 3 students had attended another of the district's elementary schools. The remaining 2 were the sole students from their 1991–92 schools.

Mr. Mayes's Class

Among the 10 classrooms I visited, the 2 with the most routinized or regularly occurring set of featured and rewarded topics and settings were the 2 at Maple Grove Elementary School. These were Mr. Mayes's and Mrs. McCartney's classes.[1] Mr. Mayes intended that his classroom would be a place for serious academic work. When I asked him how much emphasis he placed on teaching social skills and social knowledge relative to the emphasis he placed on developing students' academic skills and cognitive knowledge, he responded that he put more emphasis on academic matters. He said that he was aware that his style was probably contrary to some current trends in education, but that a combination of his own years of experience and the preferences communicated by parents had convinced him to maintain what he described as a traditional and conservative approach in his teaching. This traditional and conservative approach entailed a demand for discipline and order in the classroom, and a lot of regularity and rigor in academic matters.

It was common in Mayes's class for students exhibiting good behavior or high levels of achievement to be put forth as public examples for the rest of the class to see. Also, students exhibiting poor behavior or lower levels of academic effort were likely to be publicly criticized or sanctioned. One day in April, I was observing in McCartney's room when, through the partially closed divider between Mayes's classroom and McCartney's, I heard Mr. Mayes say the following to a student, in a voice that all in his class (and I) could hear:

> What are you doing? What are you supposed to be doing? Look around you. What are other people doing? Look at Kate. What's she doing? She's making good use of her time. What is Brian doing? He's playing. He's goofing around. Do you want to model yourself after him? Beth's working hard. So is Rick.

While I was not in the classroom to observe the full context, this statement was consistent with a pattern I perceived by which students were led to measure their behavior and academic performance relative to others in the class. Many of the students themselves contributed to the atmosphere of public assessment and comparison that characterized Mayes's classroom. There was a set of two or three girls and three or four boys who were eager to peek at one another's scores or grades when a corrected test or a graded assignment was being returned by Mr. Mayes. The following conversation was typical among the students in this set:

> *Alex:* David, if I get a better score than you, will you give me a dollar?
> *David:* No.
> *Alex* (apparently not dissuaded by David's response): And if I get more than three wrong, I'll give you a dollar.

The highly public atmosphere of the classroom seemed to make some of the lower achieving students very self-conscious about their scores and grades. After students had corrected one another's spelling quizzes,

Mr. Mayes would often call students' names one at a time; in response, a student was to report the number of spelling words he or she had gotten wrong. Usually four or five students would choose to walk to Mr. Mayes and whisper their scores to him, rather than saying the scores aloud. While this saved the students from the possible embarrassment of having to announce a score aloud, the walking and whispering did not go unnoticed by the rest of the class.

Compared to most of the other classrooms I visited, Mayes's classroom was characterized by a more restricted set of topics and activities. Whereas Mr. Clark began each day by discussing local and national events, and often by encouraging students to share personal experiences, Mr. Mayes usually kept the focus within the walls of the classroom. He was not likely to share stories about his own family or his experiences. And he was not likely to encourage students to do so. Whereas Mrs. Farr and Mr. Rettinger incorporated a lot of variety into the task structure of their lessons from day to day, Mr. Mayes followed a fairly uniform routine; one week's lesson plan and schedule looked very much like the previous week's in Mayes's class.

Although Mr. Mayes generally demanded quiet and studiousness from his students, there were some exceptions to his strict demeanor. Particularly at the end of a school day, some of the girls in the class were likely to put an arm around Mr. Mayes's shoulder, tug at his fingers, or make teasing comments. One girl actually told him playfully that he had long nose hairs. Mr. Mayes might reciprocate the friendliness and familiarity by tousling someone's hair or putting his arm around a student's shoulder while answering a question. In contrast to other teachers who exhibited these friendly and familiar relationships with students, however, Mr. Mayes was noteworthy for the way he kept the instances isolated and limited.

There were some students who played very dominant roles in Mayes's class. This fact is not surprising inasmuch as Mayes's class approached the ideal type of the unidimensional class. That ideal type, as reported in Chapter 2, is characterized by a narrow range of daily activities and tendencies toward a stable and consensual status hierarchy (Rosenholtz & Rosenholtz, 1981; Simpson, 1981).

More detail will be given on the structure of peer relations in later chapters, with the analysis and discussion of the sociometric data. It will be interesting to observe in the sociometric data the way relations in Mayes's class became increasingly hierarchical as the year progressed. Further, definite factions developed during the school year, manifesting themselves in the form of distinct and closed subgroups within the class. In later chapters, I will discuss further the ways in which I think these structural patterns relate to the general climate of Mayes's classroom.

There were 25 students in Mayes's class in the spring. Two were low-SES Asian Americans, and 3 were low-SES non-Asian students—1 White, 1 African American, and 1 Native American/White. The remaining 20 students were all high-SES White students.

Twenty-two of Mayes's students had been in the school district 2 years earlier, distributed among three schools. Three is the smallest number of "source schools" within the LaCrosse district for any of the 10 classrooms in the study; this could be expected to impact how firmly entrenched a set of norms and behaviors was among the students and how much of a previously established prestige structure existed at the beginning of the school year.

Fifteen of those 22 students had attended Maple Grove in 1991–92, including 1 low-SES White student and 14 of the high-SES White students. Another group of five high-SES White students had attended another school together in 1991–92. The other 2 students were from a third school in the district.

Mrs. McCartney's Class

In contrast to Mr. Mayes's class, Mrs. McCartney's class had more low-SES non-Asian students and fewer high-SES non-Asian students. Also, McCartney's students had been more widely distributed in 1991–92. That is, they came from a larger number of "source schools."

At the time of my spring visit, there were 24 students in McCartney's classroom. One was Asian American. She was from a high-SES family, whereas every other Asian American student in the study was from a low-SES family. Eight of the 24 students were low-SES non-Asian students, including 7 White students and 1 African American. The remaining 15 students were high-SES White students.

Twenty of the 24 students had been in the school district during the 1991–92 school year. These 20 had been distributed among five different schools in that year. Twelve of McCartney's students had attended Maple Grove in 1991–92, including 2 low-SES White students and 10 high-SES White students. Four other students had attended another school together in 1991–92. The other 4 students were either the sole students from their 1991–92 schools or were accompanied by one former schoolmate.

Regarding their teaching styles and social organization of their classrooms, Mrs. McCartney and Mr. Mayes were more alike than any of the other four pairs of teachers in the study. They had been colleagues at Maple Grove for many years. They planned many of their teaching units together and, for some lessons, removed the sliding partition that separated their classrooms and taught jointly to their two classes. For mathematics, they taught jointly to the two classes almost every day for the first half of the year; for the second half of the year the joint mathematics teaching was less frequent.

Mrs. McCartney and Mr. Mayes had similar feelings about the value of homework and the importance of a teacher's not lowering expectations for a child's performance simply because the child was from a disadvantaged home situation. Specifically, I asked both teachers how they felt about the idea that assigning homework accentuates differences among students because the more advantaged students are likely to get more help and support at home than are less advantaged students. I described teachers in other school districts who, following this logic, had moved to assigning virtually no homework in order to maintain equal participation and achievement among students. Both Mrs. McCartney and Mr. Mayes responded unfavorably to such a strategy. Mrs. McCartney spoke about the importance of impressing upon all students the value of hard work and high standards. For students from disadvantaged families, specifically, she spoke about the importance of breaking the chain of weak work ethics and high dependence on handouts.

Despite their similarities, at least two ways can be identified in which the atmosphere of McCartney's classroom differed from that of Mr. Mayes's. First, Mrs. McCartney was perhaps an even stricter disciplinarian than Mr. Mayes. Mrs. McCartney's disciplinary practices came into sharp focus for me because of a span of time when she was absent from the classroom. The substitute, who taught the class for about 6 weeks in January and February, did a very poor job of controlling the students' misbehavior. My winter visit to the classroom was during the time when the substitute was leading the class. As I watched the students, I speculated that the highly disciplined atmosphere Mrs. McCartney had established during the fall of the year would be permanently lost.

When I returned to the classroom in the spring, however, Mrs. McCartney had clearly regained order and discipline. I told her that, frankly, I was amazed. She was matter-of-fact as she explained that, upon her return in February, she told the students that, regardless of what the past 6 weeks had been like, she was back and the class would return to business as usual. Not every teacher could have regained order as Mrs. McCartney did. Her success in this realm reflected not only the priority she placed on high behavioral standards but also the thought and effort she put toward enforcing these standards.

A second way in which McCartney's class differed from Mayes's class was that her group of students did not include a core of academically dominant students to the same extent that Mayes's did. But, despite this absence, we will see in the coming chapters that some of the same tendencies toward hierarchical peer relations that characterized Mayes's class also char-acterized McCartney's class.

CLASSIFYING THE TEN CLASSROOMS

This chapter began by discussing five aspects of activity and reward structure. These were (1) teacher personalism, (2) student personalism, (3) range of performance settings, (4) rigor and uniformity of academic stan-dards, and (5) rigor and uniformity of disciplinary standards. Next were presented some vignettes, direct quotations from students and teachers, and other qualitative accounts which served to introduce the 10 classrooms. Now I want to explicitly classify the classrooms according to their activity and reward structures.

Table 4.3 shows each classroom characterized by either major, mod-erate, or minor emphasis on each of the five measures. For teacher person-alism, five classrooms—Rettinger's, Nash's, Nicholson's, Clark's, and Cavanaugh's—are coded as being characterized by a major emphasis on teacher personalism. Farr's, Rolf's, and Fredenburg's classrooms are coded as being characterized by a moderate emphasis on teacher personalism. McCartney's and Mayes's classrooms are characterized by a minor empha-sis on this trait. The pattern for student personalism is similar to that for teacher personalism, except that Fredenburg's class is coded as placing a minor emphasis on student personalism, while McCartney's class is coded as placing a moderate emphasis on this trait.

In regard to the range of performance settings, two classrooms, Rettin-ger's and Farr's, are coded as placing major emphasis on presenting a wide range. McCartney's and Mayes's classrooms are coded as placing a minor emphasis on presenting a wide range. The other six classrooms fall some-where between the extremes, placing a moderate emphasis on this trait.

As I have already suggested, the first three measures presented in Table 4.3 can be taken together to describe, roughly and loosely, the range of featured and rewarded topics and settings in each classroom. Summing the check marks for each classroom in the first three rows of the table pro-vides an approximate ranking of the classrooms from the widest to the narrowest range of featured and rewarded topics and settings. According to such a summing, Rettinger's classroom offered the widest range while Mayes's classroom offered the narrowest range. This is the order in which the classrooms are listed from left to right in Table 4.3. This ordering of the classrooms will be useful in the next chapter.

The last two rows of Table 4.3 show each classroom characterized according to the final two measures: high and uniform academic standards

Table 4.3. Descriptors of classroom activity and reward structure

Descriptor	Teacher									
	Rettinger	Nash	Nicholson	Clark	Cavanaugh	Farr	Rolf	Fredenburg	McCartney	Mayes
Teacher Personalism	✓✓	✓✓	✓✓	✓✓	✓✓	✓	✓	✓		
Student Personalism	✓✓	✓✓	✓✓	✓✓	✓✓	✓	✓		✓	
Wide Range of Performance Settings	✓✓	✓	✓	✓	✓	✓✓	✓	✓		
High and Uniform Academic Standards	✓		✓	✓	✓	✓✓	✓	✓	✓✓	✓✓
High and Uniform Disciplinary Standards	✓		✓	✓	✓	✓✓	✓	✓✓	✓✓	✓✓

Key: ✓✓ = Major emphasis; ✓ = Moderate emphasis; __ = Minor emphasis and high and uniform disciplinary standards. A first glance at these measures might suggest that they capture something absolutely antithetical to the first three measures in the table. While this is close to true, the story is not quite so simple.

Nash's, Farr's, and Rolf's classrooms disrupt the notion that the rankings suggested by the table's first three rows are simply reversed in the last two rows. While Nash's classroom looks similar to Nicholson's, Clark's, and Cavanaugh's in its range of featured and rewarded topics and settings, it is characterized by notably lower and less uniform academic and disciplinary standards than are those other three. While Farr's classroom is ranked as being in the middle of the group for the range of topics and settings, it joins McCartney's and Mayes's classrooms at the extreme for academic and disciplinary standards; these three classrooms are all characterized by high and uniform academic and disciplinary standards. Finally, Rolf's classroom is noteworthy for its minor emphasis on academic rigor and uniformity and its moderate emphasis on disciplinary rigor and uniformity. The fact that the measures in the last two rows of Table 4.3 are not perfectly antithetical to, or perfectly negatively correlated with, the measures in the first three rows adds empirical richness to the investigation of how these five classroom traits interact in impacting social relations among students.

NOTE

1. After the time of my visits to the classrooms, as I was completing the writing of this book, I had further conversations with Mr. Mayes and Mrs. McCartney. While they accepted some of my characterizations of their classrooms and their school, there were points with which they disagreed, or which they wished to supplement. Specifically, Mrs. McCartney questioned my description of her classroom as one in which the students' and the teacher's experiences away from school were not drawn upon frequently in lessons. She felt that during my three relatively short spans of observation in her classroom, I may have gotten a nonrepresentative view of what occurred in the class throughout the school year. While my scheduling of the visits in fall, winter, and spring was intended to guard against extreme biases, I acknowledge that my understanding of the classrooms was not as complete as it would have been if I had been present every day for a complete school year. Further, Mr. Mayes questioned whether I should draw evidence from an exchange I heard from the next room (described in subsequent paragraphs), when I was not present to witness the full context. He agreed that the presentation of this exchange might be

acceptable if I made clear that I was in the next room when I heard it, and that I was drawing upon it to illustrate a pattern I had observed more generally.

Both teachers expressed pride in Maple Grove's strong reputation for the quality of education it provided. To the extent that my observations of a strict disciplinary climate were accurate, the teachers noted that the presence of a visitor in the classroom would have played a role, as they sought to impress upon the students the appropriate way to behave in front of a guest. To the extent that my observations of a fairly routinized set of tasks and learning settings were accurate, Mrs. McCartney and Mr. Mayes noted that their school was very much attuned to academic standards established by the district, and that their principal periodically visited classrooms to observe adherence to these standards. Although I did not notice that this final point was more pronounced at Maple Grove than at the other schools I visited, I respectfully note the teachers' comments and present them to the reader for consideration.

5

A First Look at Peer Relations: Hierarchy and Egalitarianism

The last chapter ended by ranking the 10 classrooms according to five aspects of their activity and reward structures. A central purpose of this book is to investigate ways that activity and reward structure, and a teacher's leadership style, may affect peer relations. With this purpose in mind, I begin this chapter with three propositions about influences on the shape or structure of students' preferences.

PREDICTING THE SHAPE OF PEER RELATIONS

Proposition 1

With increased personalism and a wider range of performance settings, students will get to know one another on more dimensions. They will see more aspects of one another's interests and personalities. High levels of personalism and a wide range of performance settings should decrease the relevance of ascriptive traits such as gender, race, and socioeconomic status as students name their favorite workmates and playmates. In contrast, low levels of personalism and a narrow range of performance settings should increase the salience of ascriptive traits as students name their preferences.

Proposition 2

Assuming that students differ in their particular strengths and interests—that is, assuming different students are good at different things—a wide range of featured and rewarded topics and performance settings will allow different students to gain attention and public praise at different times. Therefore, relatively egalitarian peer relations should be expected in classrooms with a wide range of topics and performance settings.

By *egalitarian*, I mean a classroom in which most students are named as friends and desired workmates by at least some of their classmates. There would not be great discrepancies in the popularity of different students. The opposite extreme is a *hierarchical* classroom in which there are a few highly popular students receiving very large numbers of nominations as friends and desired workmates, followed by another set of moderately popular students, and a third set of students who are seldom or never named as friends and desired workmates. So, if relatively egalitarian peer relations should be expected in classrooms with a wide range of topics and performance settings, conversely, a more hierarchical arrangement should be expected in classrooms with a narrow range of topics and settings.

Proposition 3

High and uniform academic and disciplinary standards should have some tendency to foster hierarchical peer relations because—assuming a classroom's students vary in their academic abilities and behavioral patterns—some students will consistently be seen succeeding and receiving praise while other students will consistently be seen failing and receiving criticism. However, the effects of high and uniform standards should be especially strong when these standards are combined with a narrow range of topics and performance settings. The reason for this prediction is that a narrow range of topics and settings will augment the tendency for some students to succeed and gain praise consistently, while other students repeatedly fail and receive criticism. A metaphor that may be useful in thinking about this proposition is this: if the same game is played every day and all players are judged by the same high standards, it will become obvious to all which players are the stars of the game and which are not.

DISTRIBUTIONS OF WORKMATE NOMINATIONS IN FALL AND SPRING

Assessing the first proposition given above requires a consideration of individual traits in conjunction with each person's position in a network of students. This will be done in Chapters 6 and 7. Before moving to that level of detail, however, some insights can be gained by simply examining the distributions of workmate nominations made by each classroom's students in the fall of 1993 and spring of 1994. A look at these distributions allows me to make initial assessments of the second and third propositions.

Students were asked, in the fall and spring, to name two classmates with whom they would like to work on a science project. They were asked to name people who simultaneously satisfied the following: (1) people with whom they would enjoy working and (2) people with whom they would do a good job. This joint criterion was meant to elicit nominations of students who were liked and who also were seen as conforming to the classroom's model of a good and successful student. (Admittedly, it would have been interesting to isolate the two statuses—the liked classmates and the classmates with whom a student could be successful. Asking students to offer separate nominations for each of these, however, was impractical.)

These nominations can indicate which classrooms had hierarchical peer relations and which had more egalitarian relations. As described above, a hierarchically organized classroom would include a few students who received a disproportionately large number of nominations, another set who received a moderate number of nominations, and another group who were named seldom or never. A more egalitarian classroom would have the nominations more evenly distributed among students.

Because the classes had different numbers of students and because different numbers of nominations were made in each class, examining the raw number of students receiving no nominations, the number receiving two nominations, the number receiving five nominations, and the like, for each classroom is not the best way to compare the 10 classrooms. Instead, a couple of useful descriptive tools can be used. These are the *Lorenz curve* and the *Gini coefficient*. This graphical display and descriptive index are often used to depict distributions of income or wealth (Marsh, 1988). For example, if one wanted to know whether wealth was distributed more evenly among citizens in the United States or Japan, one could compare Lorenz curves and Gini coefficients for these two countries. But, more generally, these tools are useful anytime one wants to describe the distribution of a finite resource among the members of a bounded population. In this study, they can be used to describe the distribution of workmate nominations among the students in a classroom.

A Lorenz curve plots the cumulative percentage of the population receiving the resource against the cumulative share of the resource that is being received. In this study, that means plotting the cumulative proportion of all nominations received by the least popular student, the two least popular students, the three least popular students, and so on, until all of the nominations made have been accounted for.

Figures 5.1 through 5.10 show Lorenz curves for the 10 classrooms. Each figure includes a plotted curve for the distribution of workmate nominations in the fall and a second plotted curve for the distribution in the spring. There is also a straight line in each figure. This is the line of complete equality. This line depicts a hypothetical distribution of workmate nominations that is absolutely egalitarian: The first 5% of the students receive 5% of the nominations, the first 50% of the students receive 50% of the nominations, the first 90% of the students receive 90% of the nominations, and so on.

A detailed examination of Figure 5.4 will make clearer the construction and interpretation of the Lorenz curves. This particular figure, for Clark's class, is a useful example because its fall and spring curves do not overlap very much, thus making each data point easy to see. Clark's class comprised 18 students in the spring. Of these students, 1 received no nominations as a preferred workmate; 5 received one nomination each; 9 received two nominations; 1 received three nominations; and 2 students received four nominations each. Thirty-four nominations were made in all.

The first spring data point in Figure 5.4, in the lower left-hand corner of the graph, simply establishes the origin of the Lorenz curve at the point (0,0). This indicates that 0% of the nominations are accounted for by 0% of

Figure 5.1. Lorenz curves of Fall and Spring workmate nominations in Rettinger's class

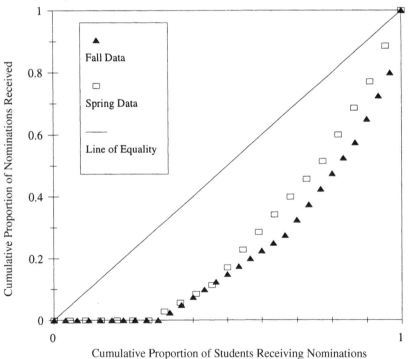

Figure 5.2. Lorenz curves of Fall and Spring workmate nominations in Nash's class

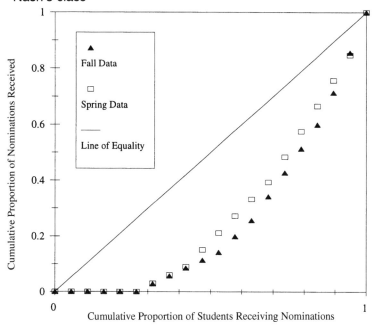

Figure 5.3. Lorenz curves of Fall and Spring workmate nominations in Nicholson's class

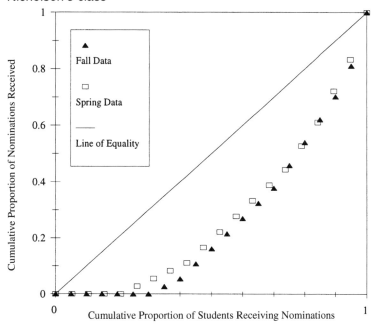

Figure 5.4. Lorenz curves of Fall and Spring workmate nominations in Clark's class

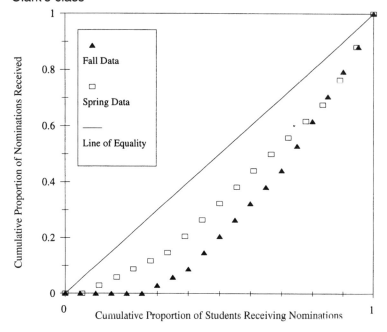

Figure 5.5. Lorenz curves of Fall and Spring workmate nominations in Cavanaugh's class

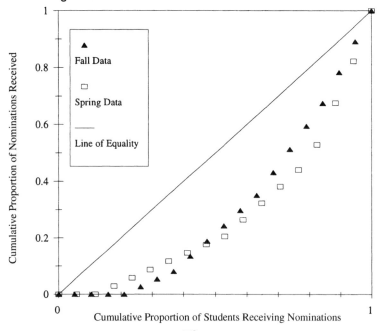

Figure 5.6. Lorenz curves of Fall and Spring workmate nominations in Farr's class

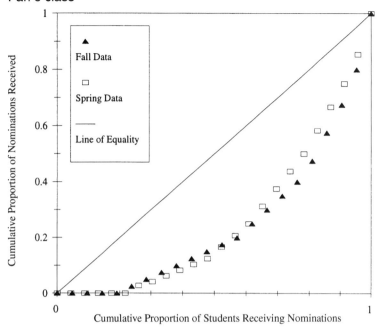

Figure 5.7. Lorenz curves of Fall and Spring workmate nominations in Rolf's class

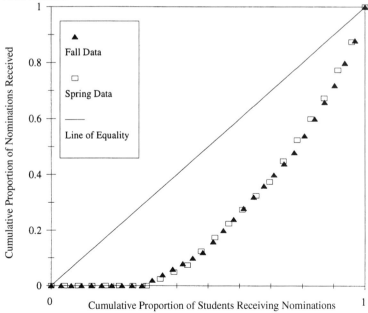

Figure 5.8. Lorenz curves of Fall and Spring workmate nominations in Fredenburg's class

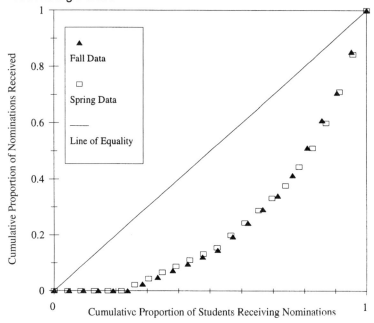

Figure 5.9. Lorenz curves of Fall and Spring workmate nominations in McCartney's class

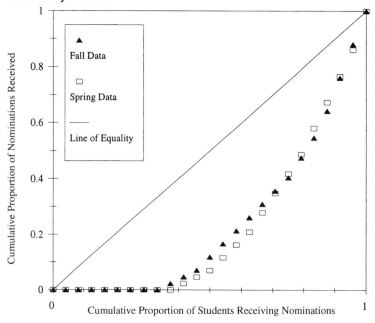

Figure 5.10. Lorenz curves of Fall and Spring workmate nominations in Mayes's class

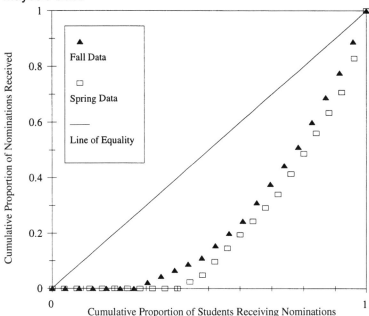

the students. Moving to the right and upward on the graph, the subsequent data points are derived by plotting students and their received nominations cumulatively as proportions of the total numbers of students and nominations. Note, then, that there are 18 spring data points after the initial one at (0,0). These 18 points account for Clark's 18 students and the workmate nominations they received.

The plotting begins with the student who received the fewest nominations, or—in terms more commonly associated with Lorenz curves and Gini coefficients—the individual with the smallest share of the finite resource. Thus, the second spring data point reflects the single student who received no nominations. This point shows that by the time I have accounted for 1 of the 18 students (or 5.6% on the horizontal axis), I have accounted for none of the 34 received nominations (or 0.0% on the vertical axis). The next five spring data points reflect the cumulative proportions realized as we introduce the 5 students who received single nominations. Thus, the seventh spring data point shows that by the time I have accounted for 6 of the 18 students (33.3%), I have accounted for 5 of the 34 nominations (14.7%). The next nine data points account for the 9 students who garnered 2 nominations apiece. Thus, when I have accounted for 15 of the 18 students, I have accounted for 23 of 34 nominations (67.6%). The next point accounts for the student who received 3 nominations, and with this student 16 of the 18 students (88.9%) had garnered 26 of the 34 nominations (76.5%). Finally, the last two data points tally the 2 students who received 4 nominations apiece. With the final spring data point, 100% of the students and 100% of the nominations have been tallied.

The fact that none of the curves of plotted data in Figures 5.1 through 5.10 follows the line of complete equality shows that each classroom had a somewhat unequal distribution of nominations in both fall and spring. Given this fact, the extent to which each plotted curve deviates from the line of equality needs to be examined. How far was each classroom from complete egalitarianism? Was each classroom's movement between fall and spring toward more egalitarian peer relations or toward more hierarchical relations?

Gini coefficients can be used in examining the degree to which the plotted lines deviate from the line of equality. To understand the interpretation of a Gini coefficient, consider the triangle formed by the line of equality, the axis at the bottom of the graph, and the axis at the right side of the graph. The proportion of this triangle that is above the plotted Lorenz curve represents the degree of inequality in the distribution, and is expressed by a Gini coefficient. Gini coefficients vary between zero and one. The coefficient for the line of complete equality would be zero. Coefficients get nearer to one as the amount of inequality increases.

The Gini coefficients for the fall and spring data of Figures 5.1 through 5.10 are tabulated in Table 5.1 and plotted in Figure 5.11. What do they reveal about the 10 classrooms? First, notice that, in both the table and the figure, the classrooms are arrayed according to their ranking from widest to narrowest range of featured and rewarded topics and performance settings. This was the rank order established in Table 4.3 in the last chapter. If Proposition 2 has some validity, there should be evidence that classrooms like Rettinger's and Nash's tended toward more egalitarian relations while classrooms like McCartney's and Mayes's tended toward more hierarchical relations.

There is no apparent relationship between this "topics and settings" ranking and the level of inequality in the fall distribution. Illustrating this point, the two highest Gini coefficients for the fall distributions are found at opposite extremes of the continuum. These are the distributions for Rettinger's class and McCartney's class. Recall that the fall data collection was in the 5th week of the school year. Any effect of classroom organization and teaching style would have been minimal that early in the school year.

Table 5.1. Gini coefficients for distributions of Fall and Spring workmate nominations

Teacher	Gini Coefficient		
	Fall	Spring	(Spring–Fall)
Rettinger	0.53	0.44	-0.09
Nash	0.49	0.44	-0.05
Nicholson	0.48	0.44	-0.04
Clark	0.40	0.27	-0.13
Cavanaugh	0.39	0.44	+0.05
Farr	0.50	0.48	-0.02
Rolf	0.48	0.47	-0.01
Fredenburg	0.51	0.50	-0.01
McCartney	0.52	0.54	+0.02
Mayes	0.48	0.56	+0.08

Better indicators of the effects of classroom organization and teaching style on the distribution of nominations are found in the spring coefficients and the change from fall to spring. An examination of the spring coefficients shows that Rettinger's, Nash's, Nicholson's, and Cavanaugh's classes are all 0.44. These four classrooms, plus Clark's, had the widest ranges of topics and performance settings. The extremely low spring coefficient for Clark's class (0.27) calls for additional explanation; it will receive more attention in Chapters 6 and 7. The classes with the narrower ranges of topics and performance settings show a steady rise in the level of the spring coefficients. The highest is for Mayes's class (0.56).

An examination of the change in the Gini coefficients between fall and spring tells basically the same story. The greatest decreases in inequality were in classrooms with relatively wide ranges of topics and performance settings. Clark's and Rettinger's classrooms showed the greatest decreases. The fact that Clark's class had a low fall coefficient and a considerable decrease suggests more than simply a convergence to some intermediate value for all of the classrooms.

Increases in Gini coefficients between fall and spring are seen for Cavanaugh's, McCartney's, and Mayes's classes. The increase for Cavanaugh's class will require further attention in Chapters 6 and 7. It is especially interesting in conjunction with the aforementioned low spring coefficient for Clark's class; Clark and Cavanaugh both taught at Campus

Figure 5.11. Gini coefficients for distributions of Fall and Spring workmate nominations

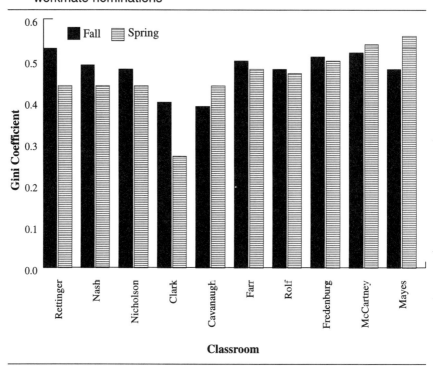

Edge and had similar teaching styles and classroom organizations. This suggests that differences in the composition of the two classes' students may be having an effect, which is exactly what will be examined in the next chapters.

The findings reviewed above provide initial support for Proposition 2. Is there also support for the third proposition? A good test would require examining a set of classrooms that had in common high and uniform academic and disciplinary standards but differed greatly in their ranges of topics and performance settings, and examining another set of classrooms that had in common low and varying standards but differed in their ranges of topics and performance settings.

The three classrooms with the highest and most uniform standards are Farr's, McCartney's, and Mayes's. Of the three, Farr's class stands apart as having the widest range of topics and performance settings. It is true that

McCartney's and Mayes's classes have higher spring coefficients than does Farr's class, as well as showing increasing inequality between fall and spring, whereas Farr's class shows a decrease in inequality. This is some evidence that, among classrooms with high and uniform standards, a narrower range of topics and performance settings is associated with a more hierarchical structure of social relations. Unfortunately, this study does not really have the right set of cases for making a corresponding assessment of the association between the range of topics and settings and the level of hierarchy in social relations among classrooms with low and varying standards. Thus there is only sparse and partial support for Proposition 3.

CONCLUSION

This chapter made use of the conceptual framework for activity and reward structures for a first look at the sociometric data. This framework will inform the investigations of Chapters 6 and 7, as well. There is initial evidence that a wide range of featured and rewarded topics and performance settings is associated with movement toward relatively egalitarian social relations, whereas a narrow range of topics and performance settings is associated with movement toward more hierarchical relations. Also, it was suggested that there should be an interaction of high levels of academic and disciplinary rigor and uniformity with the range of topics and settings as these impact social relations, although this proposition was not able to be assessed fully.

This chapter looked at workmate nominations. The other major type of social tie to be analyzed—playmate nominations—will be added to the investigations in the coming chapters. Also added in the next chapters will be individual characteristics, with an eye toward how these affect popularity and social position. And the next chapters will investigate subgroups or cliques within the classrooms. While this chapter has considered social relations as being more or less egalitarian, more or less hierarchical, with the classroom viewed as a network, the internal structures of subgroups should be considered in the same way. I now turn to these more proximate, more tightly knit, peer environments.

6

More on Peer Relations: Cohesive Subgroups

A major part of understanding the character and dynamics of a classroom's social relations is understanding the interpersonal alliances and allegiances that it contains. Cohesive subgroups, cliques within which affective preferences and friendships are concentrated, are the principal loci of the alliances and allegiances that form among a classroom's students. In this chapter, I examine the memberships and structures of the 10 classrooms' workmate and playmate subgroups.

Chapter 4 presented a conceptual framework for classifying each teacher's style and each classroom's social organization. Chapter 5 presented three propositions regarding the relationship between activity and reward structures and the structure of peer relations. These propositions should be true for the internal structures of cohesive subgroups just as they were hypothesized to hold true for the larger networks of whole classrooms. In this chapter I investigate the propositions at the level of the subgroup.

The three propositions made predictions about the salience of ascriptive characteristics in students' preferences of workmates and playmates and about the degree of hierarchy (or, conversely, egalitarianism) that characterized peer relations. In addition to those network features, this chapter introduces two other structural characteristics: subgroup closure and subgroup in-degree. These will be defined and discussed in the coming pages.

In examining the salience of ascriptive characteristics, I investigate subgroup memberships. Which students clustered together? Did students who shared gender, socioeconomic status, race, or enrollment histories gravitate toward one another as workmates and playmates, or were the cliques heterogeneous with respect to these traits? Proposition 1 of Chapter 5 predicted that students' ascriptive characteristics should have guided workmate and playmate preferences least strongly in classrooms characterized by high levels of personalism and wide ranges of performance settings. Specifically, ascriptive characteristics should have been least salient in Rettinger's, Nash's, Nicholson's, Clark's, and Cavanaugh's classrooms as the school year proceeded. In contrast, ascriptive traits should have been most salient in Mayes's, McCartney's, and Fredenburg's classrooms.

In returning to the investigation of egalitarianism versus hierarchy, I ask whether a clique comprised a set of students who all received similar numbers of nominations from their fellow subgroup members or, alternatively, comprised a few highly popular individuals with a following of admirers. Gini coefficients are used once again to measure the degree to which students' nominations of workmates and playmates were evenly distributed among the members of each subgroup. In Chapter 5, Gini coefficients were used to describe the distribution of workmate nominations within each of the 10 classrooms, considered as a whole. In this chapter, a Gini coefficient is calculated for each subgroup, based only upon the nominations that remained within the subgroup.

Proposition 2 of Chapter 5 predicted that the classrooms with the widest ranges of featured and rewarded topics and performance settings would have tended toward relatively egalitarian structures, whereas classrooms with narrow ranges of topics and performance settings would have tended toward relatively hierarchical structures. Again, the classrooms with the widest ranges of topics and performance settings were Rettinger's, Nash's, Nicholson's, Clark's, and Cavanaugh's. The classrooms with the narrowest ranges of topics and performance settings were Mayes's, McCartney's, and Fredenburg's.

Proposition 3 predicted that the tendency toward hierarchical structures would have been especially strong when a narrow range of topics and performance settings was coupled with high and uniform academic and disciplinary standards. As was the case in Chapter 5, the ability to test this hypothesis is limited, but I will compare the degree of hierarchy within subgroups among Farr's, McCartney's, and Mayes's classes. These three classes shared major emphases on academic and disciplinary rigor and uniformity. Farr's class contrasted with McCartney's and Mayes's, however, in that it was characterized by a wider range of topics and performance settings. If the students in Farr's class tended to be located in less hierarchically structured subgroups than were the students in the other two classes, this will be some support for Proposition 3.

In addition to an assessment of the three propositions from Chapter 5, this chapter's consideration of subgroup structures and memberships includes other important issues. For example, where hierarchical subgroups existed, it is important to ask which students were central and which were peripheral. Were certain ascriptive traits associated with centrality within the clique? Did other traits characterize the peripheral members?

Further considering the structure of the subgroups, I examine their degree of closure. *Closure* is defined as the proportion of all nominations extended by a subgroup's members that remained within the subgroup. If all of the nominations extended by a subgroup's members remained within the subgroup, it was indeed a tightly knit and self-contained clique. On the other hand, if several of the nominations extended by a subgroup's members were sent to members of other cliques, then the subgroup was a less rigidly delineated entity. If closure was low for all or most of a classroom's subgroups, this may be evidence of a pattern of social relations that was still evolving. Alternatively, this may be evidence of a social system in which the strongest allegiances and identifications were with the whole group (the whole class) rather than with cliques within the class. No a priori propositions are offered about which classrooms would display relatively closed subgroups, but the data will reveal patterns that add to an understanding of peer relations in the 10 classrooms. The patterns will suggest hypotheses that can be tested in future research.

Finally, for classrooms in which there were considerable numbers of between-subgroup nominations, it is enlightening to note which cliques' members were most frequently the recipients of nominations from other cliques. In investigating this structural feature of subgroups, I utilize a measure called in-degree. *In-degree* is defined as the proportion of other subgroups' nominations that were received by the members of the subgroup in question. For example, an in-degree of 0.20 for subgroup X means that the members of X received, on average, 20% of the nominations initiated by members of any one of the other subgroups in the classroom. A subgroup that is high on this measure is one whose members were popular or admired by others in the larger network. By considering the in-degrees of a classroom's cliques, one can identify whether there were one or more cliques that were especially central to the classroom's social structure. Again, there are no a priori propositions to test regarding in-degree, but explanations of the observed patterns and hypotheses for future investigation can be developed inductively.

In considering the empirical patterns, I give special attention to changes that occurred between fall and spring of the school year. Changes which occurred during the year indicate the direction of the evolution of a classroom's social relations. In accordance with this fact, I again try to link each classroom's direction of change and final state with the activity and reward structures of the classroom, in conjunction with the broader context of the school and the traits of the students in the classroom.

I will begin with a description of the algorithm used to identify cohesive subgroups, next give an illustration that compares workmate cliques in Nash's and McCartney's classes, and then proceed to an investigation of the three propositions from Chapter 5 as well as closure and in-degree at the subgroup level.

IDENTIFYING COHESIVE SUBGROUPS

Various techniques have been used to identify cohesive subgroups from social network data (see reviews in Frank, 1995; Hallinan, 1980). Frank has developed the *KliqueFinder* algorithm for this task. KliqueFinder operates upon data arranged in a traditional "chooser-chosen" matrix in which the *ij*th entry represents the strength of the tie going from person *i* to person *j*. With KliqueFinder, individuals are iteratively reassigned to subgroups so as to maximize a function associated with the probability that two people interact if they are members of the same subgroup. The result is the identification of a set of maximally cohesive, nonoverlapping subgroups between which ties may exist but within which most ties are concentrated. Each person in the data set will either be identified as a social isolate or will be assigned to one and only one subgroup within which most of the ties to and from him or her are concentrated.

An important feature of KliqueFinder is the calculation of a goodness-of-fit statistic that tests the derived subgroup assignments against the null hypothesis that people initiate exchanges with others randomly, without regard for subgroup boundaries. That is, after the algorithm has identified maximally cohesive subgroups, one can assess the probability that the observed concentration of ties within subgroups could occur due to chance alone, if the subgroups were essentially meaningless. This assessment is necessary because KliqueFinder, like other clustering algorithms, will identify clusters even in random data.

For the LaCrosse data, KliqueFinder was used to identify cohesive subgroups for workmate preferences within each of the 10 classrooms in both fall and spring. In responding to the question about students with whom they would like to work on a science project, respondents were asked to limit their nominations to others in the classroom. The classroom was a natural and reasonable boundary as students considered their preferred workmates. Thus, in light of the way the question was posed, each classroom can be analyzed as a bounded network for workmate preferences.

In contrast, in responding to the question about students with whom they usually played at recess, respondents were invited to name anyone in the school. The great majority of nominees were other fourth graders. Nominees were most often students from the same classroom as the nominator. But, reflecting students' actual patterns of play, a substantial minority of the playmate nominations went to students from a classroom other than the nominator's classroom. In a decision that eliminated from consideration a small number of students who were nominated as playmates, only nominations sent to students in one of the study's 2 classrooms per school were submitted to the KliqueFinder algorithm. The benefit of this decision, however, was that data about ascriptive characteristics, as well as qualitative observations, were available for everyone assigned to one of the resulting subgroups. In light of the question asked of the students, each pair of 2 classrooms per school—rather than each of the 10 classrooms—was analyzed as a bounded network for playmate relations. As with the workmate subgroups, playmate subgroups were identified for both fall and spring.

Meaningful subgroup structures were found via KliqueFinder. For each of the 20 workmate networks analyzed (10 classrooms in fall and spring), there was enough evidence to reject the null hypothesis that individuals made their nominations independent of the identified subgroups ($p < .001$). For each of the 10 playmate networks (five schools in fall and spring), the null hypothesis was also rejected ($p < .001$). The subgroups identified among the students represent a real empirical tendency for students' preferred workmates and usual playmates to be concentrated within the identified subgroup boundaries.

TWO CLASSROOMS COMPARED: AN ILLUSTRATION

Once cohesive subgroups have been identified with KliqueFinder, the interactions within and between the cliques can be mapped. Frank (1993, 1996) discusses ways to construct these sociograms via multidimensional scaling (MDS) techniques.

To begin this chapter's analysis and discussion of the subgroups in the 10 classrooms, this section presents MDS-based sociograms for the workmate subgroups in 2 of the classrooms, Nash's and McCartney's. The plots from these 2 classrooms are offered as initial illustrations. The discussion of these plots highlights some of the issues that are central to understanding the evolution of subgroup structures in the 10 classrooms. Specifically, hierarchy, closure, in-degree, and the salience of ascriptive traits such as gender, race, and SES will be discussed.

Figures 6.1 through 6.4 depict the structure of workmate subgroups for Nash's and McCartney's classes in the fall and in the spring. The four figures together illustrate the fact that these two classrooms had similar structures of workmate subgroups in the fall but had very different structures in the spring. The propositions of the last chapter and our qualitative understandings of Nash's and McCartney's classes take us a long way in understanding why these two classes diverged from one another in their patterns of social relations.

Figure 6.1 shows that Nash's class had five workmate subgroups in the fall. These cliques are demarcated by the five solid circles and are labeled "A," "B," "C," "D," and "E." Each student is represented by an iden-

Figure 6.1. Fall workmate nominations within and between cohesive subgroups in Nash's class

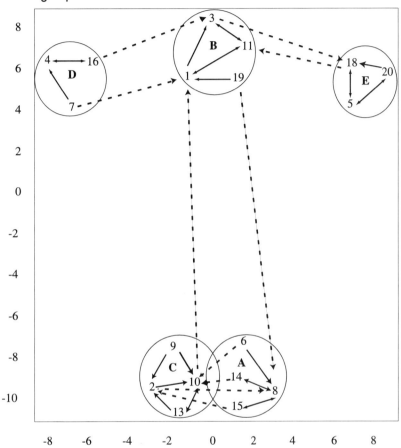

tification number (e.g., student #2 in subgroup C or student #20 in subgroup E).

The two axes of the figure are empirically determined, underlying dimensions. Because of the way they are derived by the multidimensional scaling procedure, the two dimensions of a sociogram generally do not correspond directly to anything as concrete as a subgroup's average socioeconomic status or where students sat in the classroom. Rather they are derived as the best way to give a two-dimensional representation of the distance between any pair of students, or any pair of subgroups, so that the distance between them in the sociogram is inversely related to the

Figure 6.2. Spring workmate nominations within and between cohesive subgroups in Nash's class

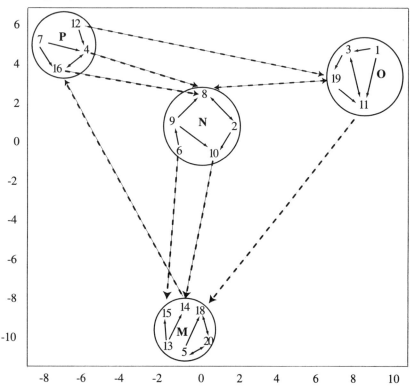

strength of their association with one another. Thus, a small distance between two students, or two subgroups, represents the fact that the link between them is relatively strong, either through direct ties, indirect ties, or a combination of these. A large distance between two students or subgroups represents a weak relationship between the two. Generally, two students or subgroups that are very far from one another will not be linked by any direct ties and, perhaps, not even by indirect ties. One exception to this general claim is the case of two students who are in different subgroups but who share a tie (e.g., #19 in subgroup B and #8 in subgroup A in Figure 6.1). In this case, the considerable distance between the students is a function of the dearth of other ties between their respective subgroups in addition to the one tie that #19 extends to #8.

As the previous paragraph suggested, it is often difficult to attach qualitative interpretations to the horizontal and vertical dimensions of a sociogram other than a vague notion of "social distance." In the case of Figure 6.1, however, the composition of the five subgroups suggests that the vertical dimension corresponds quite directly to gender. For the reader to understand this, I need to share the information that subgroups A and C, at the bottom of the plot, each consisted of four girls. Subgroups D and E each consisted of three boys, while subgroup B consisted of three boys and a girl. These latter three subgroups are located near the top of the plot. In addition to the 18 students assigned to these five subgroups, one boy who made only a single nomination and received no nominations was removed from the analysis as an isolate.

There was a moderate amount of nominating between the subgroups. Each interclique nomination is indicated by a dotted line in the sociogram, with an arrow pointing toward the recipient of the nomination. The members of subgroup A sent three nominations to members of subgroup C (#6 to #10, #14 to #10, and #15 to #2). One member of B sent a nomination to a member of A (#19 to #8) while another sent a nomination to a member of E (#3 to #18). Similarly, one member of C sent a nomination to a member of A (#2 to #8), while another sent a nomination to a member of B (#10 to #1). The members of D sent two nominations to B (#16 to #3, and #7 to #1) while one member of E sent a nomination to a member of B (#18 to #11).

The internal structures of the subgroups in Nash's class were characterized by a moderate degree of hierarchy, with a subgroup's degree of hierarchy being measured by a Gini coefficient as discussed earlier. In the plot, nominations within cliques are indicated by solid lines with an arrow pointing toward the recipient; a double-headed arrow indicates reciprocated nominations. The most hierarchical clique was subgroup A, in which a high-SES White girl (#8) received three nominations from other clique members; a low-SES White girl (#14) and a low-SES Asian American girl (#15) received one nomination apiece; and another low-SES White girl (#6) received no nominations from other clique members. The least hierarchical was subgroup E, in which the low-SES Asian American boys (#18, #5, and #20) who constituted the clique received two, two, and one nominations from other clique members, respectively.

Subgroup C consisted entirely of high-SES White girls. Subgroup E consisted of all low-SES Asian American boys. The other three cliques were internally heterogeneous with respect to race and SES. So, in summary, the subgroup structure in Nash's class in the fall was characterized by strong but not complete gender segregation, a moderate amount of interclique nominating, a moderate degree of hierarchy, and some tendency toward grouping according to SES and race. Given this structure, what did the class look like in the spring?

Figure 6.2 shows the workmate subgroup structure for Nash's class in the spring. The four identified subgroups are labeled "M," "N," "O," and "P." All of Nash's students were assigned to subgroups; none were removed from the analysis as isolates. Again, a moderate number of nominations were sent between cliques. Every subgroup had some tie to every other; at the minimum, each group either sent one nomination to, or received one nomination from, every other group.

Gender, race, and SES were not as strongly tied to subgroup membership as they had been for this class in the fall. Subgroups M and O were both heterogeneous with respect to gender. Every subgroup except for N contained both Asian American and non-Asian students. Every subgroup except for P contained both high-SES and low-SES students.

The degree of hierarchy within the subgroups was slightly greater, on average, than it had been in the fall. The most hierarchical subgroup was P, with its low-SES Asian American members (#4, #16, and #12) receiving three, two, and zero nominations from other subgroup members, respectively, while its sole low-SES White member (#7) received zero nominations from other members. Note that a student could be assigned to a subgroup if he or she received no nominations from other subgroup members, as long as he or she extended nominations. This explains why students #7 and #12 were included as members of subgroup P, albeit peripheral ones whose nominations were not reciprocated. Individuals were only identified as isolates if their inclusion in a subgroup lowered the criterion being maximized by the KliqueFinder algorithm, which generally would occur only if a student's number of received nominations plus extended nominations summed to just zero or one.

The least hierarchical subgroup was M, with its members (#18, #20, #5, #14, #15, and #13) receiving two, two, one, one, one, and zero nominations, respectively. The members of subgroup M who received two nominations were both low-SES Asian American boys (#18 and #20). The members who received one nomination were another Asian American boy (#5), an Asian American girl (#15), and a White girl (#14); each of these three students was from a low-SES family. The member who received no nominations was a high-SES White girl (#13).

The main stories in the evolution of subgroup structure in Nash's class between fall and spring were the following:

1. By spring, none of the subgroups emerged as much more central or dominant than the others.
2. Every clique had at least one tie to every other by spring.
3. Ascriptive characteristics were less closely tied to subgroup membership and to one's position within the subgroup as the year proceeded.

4. The level of hierarchy within subgroups was at a moderate level in the fall and increased only slightly by the spring.

The evolution of subgroup structure in McCartney's class between fall and spring provides a contrast. From Figure 6.3, one can see that McCartney's class shared some structural qualities with Nash's class in the fall. The six subgroups, labeled "G," "H," "I," "J," "K," and "L," were differentiated by gender, as were Nash's in the fall. The three subgroups at the bottom of the plot, G, I, and J, consisted of all girls. Subgroups K and L, at the top of the plot, consisted of all boys, while subgroup H consisted of

Figure 6.3. Fall workmate nominations within and between cohesive subgroups in McCartney's class

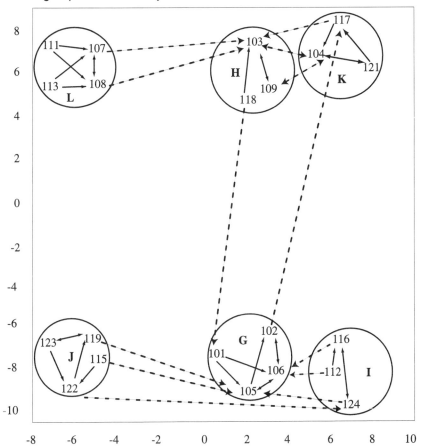

Figure 6.4. Spring workmate nominations within and between cohesive subgroups in McCartney's class

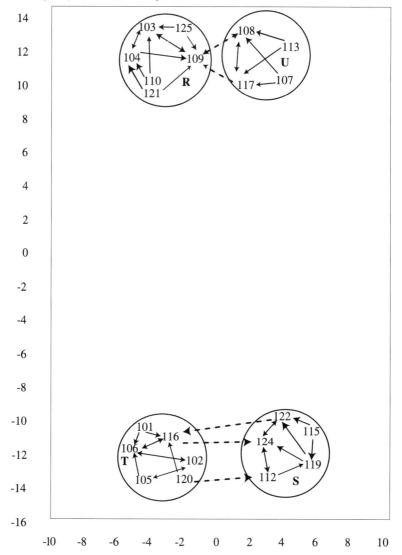

two boys and one girl. In addition to the 21 students assigned to subgroups, 3 students were removed from the analysis as isolates. These students— two low-SES White boys and a low-SES White girl—received no nominations; nominations made by them were missing data.

There was considerable nominating between subgroups, somewhat more than was observed for Nash's class in the fall. However, most of the interclique ties were among the set of three subgroups at the top of the plot or among the set of three subgroups at the bottom of the plot. Only two interclique ties (from #118 in subgroup H to #101 in subgroup G, and from #102 in subgroup G to #117 in subgroup K) cross the broad expanse that separates the two sets of subgroups.

The average degree of internal hierarchy for the six subgroups falls somewhere between what was observed for Nash's class in the fall and Nash's class in the spring. The most hierarchical subgroup among the six in McCartney's class was subgroup L. In this clique, two high-SES White boys (#107 and #108) each received three nominations from other subgroup members while a low-SES White boy (#111) and another high-SES White boy (#113) received no nominations. The least hierarchical subgroup among McCartney's six was subgroup K. In this clique consisting of all high-SES White boys, one boy (#104) received two nominations from the other subgroup members while the other two boys (#117 and #121) each received a single nomination.

The subgroups were fairly heterogeneous with respect to SES. Every clique except for I and K contained both high-SES and low-SES students. It is noteworthy that the least hierarchical subgroup was the only one that was completely homogeneous with respect to gender, race, and SES. Throughout this chapter, it will be important to note whether it was consistently true that egalitarian cliques tended to be homogeneous with respect to ascriptive characteristics while hierarchical cliques tended to be heterogeneous.

There were only two non-White students in McCartney's class. One was a high-SES Asian American girl (#116) who joined two high-SES White girls (#112 and #124) in subgroup I. The other was a low-SES African American girl (#102) who joined two low-SES White girls (#101 and #105) and a high-SES White girl (#106) in subgroup G.

Visually, one can see similarities between the plots for Nash's and McCartney's classes in the fall (Figures 6.1 and 6.3). The predominant features in each plot are a set of all-girl subgroups at the bottom of the plot with several ties between them, a set of virtually all-boy subgroups at the top of the plot with several ties between them, and just a couple of ties linking the set of cliques at the bottom with the set of cliques at the top. Given these similarities, it is natural to ask whether the evolution of subgroup structure between fall and spring for McCartney's class mirrored the evolution we observed for Nash's class.

As one observes these evolutions for the two classrooms, one should ask whether the trends observed in Nash's class can be partially explained by an understanding of that classroom as one characterized by major emphases on teacher and student personalism, a moderate emphasis on including a wide range of performance settings, and minor emphases on academic and disciplinary press and uniformity. One should ask whether the trends observed in McCartney's class can be partially explained by that classroom's relatively narrow range of featured performance settings, minor emphasis on teacher personalism, moderate emphasis on student personalism, and major emphasis on both academic and disciplinary rigor and uniformity.

A look at Figure 6.4 immediately suggests that McCartney's class did not follow an evolution that was similar to that of Nash's class. The figure shows two subgroups, labeled "R" and "U," near the top of the plot that consisted of all boys. The other two subgroups, labeled "S" and "T," near the bottom of the plot consisted of all girls. Additionally, three students were removed from the analyses as isolates.

A few ties passed between R and U; one nomination went from R to U (#109 to #108) and two went from U to R (#108 to #109, and #117 to #109). One member of S sent a nomination to T (#122 to #116) and two members of T sent nominations to S (#116 to #124, and #120 to #112). For the most part, though, the class was characterized by four dense, self-contained cliques.

These four cliques were quite hierarchical internally. The average degree of hierarchy for these four subgroups was higher than the average for the subgroups in this class in the fall. It was also higher than the average for Nash's class in either the fall or the spring. The most central students in each of the four subgroups were high-SES White students. Low-SES and non-White students were located either at less central positions within the cliques or were removed from the analysis as isolates. Not to overstate the case, however, I must point out that some high-SES White students were also in peripheral positions or, in one case, removed from the analysis as an isolate.

Overall, though, it is clear that two classrooms that had fairly similar sociometric structures early in the school year looked very different from each other by the end of the school year. Can one account for the different paths with the qualitative descriptions and the categorizations of task and reward structures of Chapter 4? To a considerable degree, one can.

Recall from Table 4.3 that Nash's class was characterized by major emphases on teacher and student personalism, and a moderate emphasis on including a wide range of performance settings. Further, it was characterized by minor emphases on academic and disciplinary rigor and uniformity. In contrast, McCartney's class was characterized by a minor emphasis on teacher personalism, a moderate emphasis on student personalism, and a minor emphasis on including a wide range of performance settings. It was categorized as placing major emphases on both academic and disciplinary rigor and uniformity.

Proposition 1 in Chapter 5 predicted that during the school year McCartney's class, in contrast to Nash's class, would tend toward a greater salience of ascriptive characteristics in students' workmate preferences. The second and third propositions predicted that McCartney's class, in contrast with Nash's, would tend toward a more hierarchical network structure, at the subgroup level as well as the classroom level. Consistent with these predictions, gender did remain highly salient in student's preferences for McCartney's class while decreasing in its salience for Nash's class. Also, in the spring the subgroups in McCartney's class tended to be more internally hierarchical than the subgroups in Nash's class were.

It is difficult to compare the two classrooms in terms of the salience of race because of their very different student compositions. One can examine the salience of SES, though. Three of the four spring workmate subgroups in each classroom were heterogeneous with respect to SES. In McCartney's class, however, the most central positions within subgroups were occupied solely by high-SES students, while this was not true for Nash's class.

I made no predictions about the closure and in-degree of subgroups within a classroom's larger network structure. Clearly, though, McCartney's class developed a set of workmate cliques with higher closure and lower in-degree than did Nash's class as the year proceeded.

The plots for Nash's and McCartney's classes illustrate some of the intricacies of subgroup structure and membership that must be examined. Certainly students' workmate preferences evolved in strikingly different ways in these two classrooms over the course of the school year. In light of the qualitative descriptions of the classrooms in Chapter 4, reasonably convincing explanations have been offered about the ways students' traits and the task and reward structure of each classroom jointly facilitated the observed patterns of workmate preferences.

One could try to develop the same types of explanations for patterns of workmate subgroups in the other 8 classrooms and for playmate subgroups in the five schools based on sociograms. Figures depicting workmate subgroups for the other 8 classrooms and figures depicting playmate subgroups for the five schools are available for interested readers upon request. However, it becomes overwhelming and unmanageable to compare the 10 classrooms via the inspection of these plots.

It is more manageable and, I think, more informative to isolate some of the key traits that characterized cliques and interclique relations and to make comparisons across schools and classrooms. Hence, it is to those tasks that I now turn.

SUBGROUP MEMBERSHIP: ASSESSING PROPOSITION 1

Did students tend to cluster in cohesive subgroups according to their ascriptive characteristics? The first proposition hypothesized that there would have been such a tendency in classrooms with low levels of personalism and narrow ranges of performance settings, whereas such a tendency would have been absent or diminished in classrooms with high levels of personalism and wide ranges of performance settings. An examination of the data, however, does not support the proposition as it relates to gender or race/SES.

Tables 6.1 through 6.4 provide a summary of the composition of the spring workmate subgroups in the 10 classrooms and the spring playmate subgroups in the five schools. Table 6.1 tabulates the workmate subgroups

Table 6.1. Tabulation of Spring workmate subgroups by classroom, indicating subgroup gender composition

	'*X*' Indicates Subgroup That Includes...		
Classroom	Boys Only	Girls Only	Both Boys and Girls
Nash	*X*	*X*	*XX*
Nicholson	*XX*	*XX*	
Clark	*XXX*	*XX*	
Cavanaugh	*XXX*	*X*	
Farr	*XX*	*X*	*XX*
Fredenburg	*XX*	*XX*	*X*
Mayes	*XX*	*XX*	
McCartney	*XX*	*XX*	
Rolf	*XX*	*XX*	*X*
Rettinger	*XX*	*X*	*X*

according to whether each contained boys only, girls only, or both boys and girls. This table shows that the majority of spring workmate subgroups comprised only one gender, either males or females. The classrooms that deviated from this trend the most were Nash's (two of four cliques were mixed by gender) and Farr's (two of five cliques were mixed by gender). The classrooms that adhered most rigidly to the trend of single-gender cliques, with all of their subgroups being single-gender, were Nicholson's, Clark's, Cavanaugh's, Mayes's, and McCartney's. While Table 6.1 shows that some classrooms adhered to single-gender workmate subgroups more rigidly than other classrooms did, personalism and the range of performance settings are not sufficient to explain these differences.

Table 6.2 tabulates the spring workmate cliques according to whether each contained (a) Asian American students only, (b) low-SES non-Asian students only, (c) high-SES non-Asian students only, (d) students from any of the three possible pairings of these categories, or (e) students from all three of these categories. Most of the cliques were heterogeneous with respect to the race / SES classification, comprising students from at least two of the three categories. Three classrooms had only heterogeneous cliques; these were Nash's, Farr's, and Fredenburg's.

In classrooms with cliques that comprised students from only one of the categories, these cliques almost always comprised high-SES non-Asian students. In fact, there were no cliques that contained low-SES non-Asian students exclusively. There was only one clique that contained Asian American students exclusively. This Asian American clique was in Clark's class. Clark's class had the most segregated workmate cliques of any of the 10 classes.

Table 6.3 tabulates the spring playmate subgroups according to gender composition. A comparison of this table with Table 6.1 shows that mixed-gender playmate cliques were somewhat more common than mixed-gender workmate cliques. Whereas only 7 of the 44 spring workmate subgroups—from all 10 classrooms—were of mixed gender, a somewhat higher proportion of the spring playmate subgroups was of mixed gender (10 of 37 playgroups).

A comparison of Tables 6.1 and 6.3 provides mixed evidence about whether patterns established in the workmate relationships of the classroom were replicated in the playmate relationships of the playground. Supporting the idea that the patterns were replicated are the facts that the two classrooms from Fawndale Elementary School—Farr's and Fredenburg's—together had three mixed-gender workmate cliques and that four of the school's nine playmate cliques were of mixed gender. Similarly, the two classrooms from Riverside Elementary School—Rolf's and Rettinger's—each had a mixed gender workmate clique and three of the

Table 6.2. Tabulation of Spring workmate subgroups by classroom, indicating subgroup racial and socioeconomic status (SES) composition

'X' Indicates Subgroup That Includes…

Classroom	Asian American Only	Low SES Non Asian Only	High SES Non Asian Only	Asian American & Low SES Non Asian	Asian American & High SES Non Asian	Low SES Non Asian & High SES Non Asian	Asian American, Low SES Non Asian, & High SES Non Asian
Nash				x		x	xx
Nicholson			x		xx	x	
Clark	x		xx		x	x	
Cavanaugh			x	x	x	x	
Farr						xxx	xx
Fredenburg					x		xxxx
Mayes			x		x	xx	
McCartney			x			xx	x
Rolf			x	x		xx	x
Rettinger			x		xx	x	

96

Table 6.3. Tabulation of Spring playmate subgroups by school, indicating subgroup gender composition

	'*X*' Indicates Subgroup That Includes…		
School	Boys Only	Girls Only	Both Boys and Girls
New Forest	*XXX*	*XXX*	
Campus Edge	*XXXX*	*X*	*XX*
Fawndale	*XX*	*XXX*	*XXXX*
Maple Grove	*XX*	*XXX*	*X*
Riverside	*XXX*	*XXX*	*XXX*

school's nine playmate cliques were of mixed gender. On the other hand, contrary to the idea that workmate patterns were replicated in playmate patterns, two of the four workmate cliques in Nash's class were of mixed gender but none of the playmate cliques at New Forest Elementary School were of mixed gender.

Finally, Table 6.4 tabulates the spring playmate subgroups according to racial and SES composition. The patterns for playmate subgroups shown in this table are quite similar to the patterns for workmate subgroups shown in Table 6.2. Most of the playmate cliques were heterogeneous with respect to the race/SES classification, comprising students from at least two of the three categories. All of the cliques at Maple Grove Elementary School were heterogeneous with respect to race/SES.

At the other four schools, cliques that comprised students from only one of the categories were cliques that comprised solely high-SES non-Asian students (in seven instances) or solely Asian American students (in two instances). As was the case with workmate cliques, there were no instances of playmate cliques comprising solely low-SES non-Asian students.

EGALITARIANISM VERSUS HIERARCHY: ASSESSING PROPOSITIONS 2 AND 3

The second and third propositions from Chapter 5 made predictions about the degree of hierarchy that characterized peer relations in the 10 classrooms. Specifically, Proposition 2 hypothesized that classrooms with a wide range of topics and performance settings would tend toward egalitarian peer relations, whereas classrooms with a narrow range would tend toward hierarchy. Proposition 3 hypothesized that high and uniform academic and disciplinary standards would foster hierarchical peer relations,

Table 6.4. Tabulation of Spring playmate subgroups by school, indicating subgroup racial and socioeconomic status (SES) composition

School				'X' Indicates Subgroup That Includes...			
	Asian American Only	Low SES Non Asian Only	High SES Non Asian Only	Asian American & Low SES Non Asian	Asian American & High SES Non Asian	Low SES Non Asian & High SES Non Asian	Asian American, Low SES Non Asian, & High SES Non Asian
New Forest	X		X	X	X	X	X
Campus Edge	X		XX	X	X	X	XX
Fawndale			XX		XX	XXX	XX
Maple Grove					X	XXXX	X
Riverside			XX	X	XX	XXXX	

and also that this tendency would be strongest when high and uniform standards were coupled with a narrow range of topics and settings.

To investigate the degree of hierarchy characterizing the internal structure of each subgroup, I first calculated the Gini coefficient for each subgroup. The median Gini coefficient for workmate subgroups, based on both fall and spring cliques, was 0.36. The median for playmate subgroups, again based on both fall and spring cliques, was somewhat lower, 0.25. Using these medians as guidelines, each subgroup could be categorized as having had a low or high Gini coefficient; that is, each could be categorized as having been below or above the grand median.

As one inspects the degree of hierarchy that characterized each classroom and assesses Propositions 2 and 3, it is important to think about the differences between these workmate cliques and playmate cliques. First, the question asked of students about desired workmates was predicated on a hypothetical science project they might do. That is, the students were not asked, "Who do you usually work with when you have the freedom to choose partners?" Rather, they were asked, "If you were doing this science project, with whom would you like to work?"

The subtle difference between the two questions is important to recognize as one compares the observed structures of workmate cliques with the observed structures of playmate cliques. The question asked of students about playmates was "Who do you usually play with at recess?" So, whereas students' responses about their playmates primarily reflected their actual friendships and associations, responses about workmates had the additional component of students' desires for friendships or associations. Some responses reflected desires that were never realized.

A second important issue to consider as one inspects the workmate and playmate cliques is that the propositions of Chapter 5 dealt with the ways a classroom's activity and reward structure affected the contexts in which students viewed one another and the parts of each student's abilities, interests, and personality that were visible to his or her classmates. It is my contention that the relationships that were formed in the classroom (where the students spent the great majority of their in-school time) carried over into other contexts, including the playground. However, the link between classroom organization and patterns of peer relations should have been strongest for peer relations rooted in the classroom. In moving from the classroom to the playground, the propositions of Chapter 5 may need modification or elaboration to account for other relevant factors.

With the preceding points in mind, look at the data for the 10 classrooms. Figure 6.5 shows, for each classroom, the proportion of students (those not removed from the analyses as isolates) who were in workmate subgroups with Gini coefficients above the grand median for workmate

Figure 6.5. Proportion of students in workmate subgroups with high Gini coefficients (isolates removed)

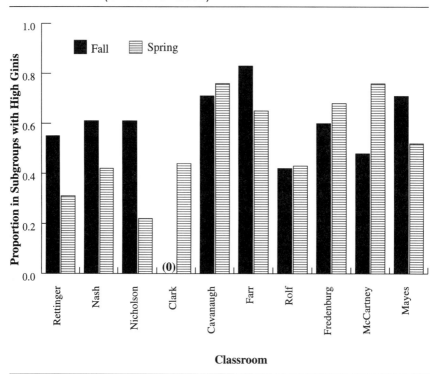

cliques (that is, above 0.36). The figure illustrates both fall and spring levels.

Similar to the findings of Chapter 5, when the distribution of nominations within each classroom considered as a whole was analyzed, the fall levels do not reveal a clear pattern as one inspects Figure 6.5 from left to right. Clark's classroom exhibited the least hierarchical workmate cliques in the fall; none of his students was in a subgroup with a high Gini coefficient. Farr's classroom exhibited the most hierarchical workmate cliques in the fall; fully 83% of her students were in subgroups with high Gini coefficients.

Whereas no clear pattern is seen for the fall levels, by spring, the rank ordering of the classrooms is fairly consistent with Proposition 2. That is, there is a tendency for the classrooms with the widest ranges of topics and performance settings to have the most egalitarian peer relations in the spring. From least hierarchical to most hierarchical the classrooms are ranked as follows: Nicholson, Rettinger, Nash, Rolf, Clark, Mayes, Farr, Fredenburg, and a tie between Cavanaugh and McCartney. The main deviations from the rank ordering that was predicted by the proposition are the relatively high degree of hierarchy in Cavanaugh's classroom and the relatively low degree of hierarchy in Mayes's classroom.

I do not have a good explanation for the low level in Mayes's classroom. There is, however, a fairly simple explanation for the high level of hierarchy in Cavanaugh's classroom. This was the one classroom among the 10 that had a very uneven gender composition. In the spring, Cavanaugh's class had 13 boys and only four girls. Each of the other classes was closer to an even division in its gender composition. It is true for all of the classrooms that all-boy subgroups tended to be considerably more hierarchically structured than either all-girl subgroups or mixed-gender subgroups. For Cavanaugh's class, all 13 boys were members of all-boy subgroups with high Gini coefficients. The four girls were members of an all-girl subgroup with a low Gini coefficient.

While Figure 6.5 offers considerable support for Proposition 2, it does not offer support for Proposition 3, which involved the interaction between high and uniform standards and a narrow range of topics and settings. As was the case in Chapter 5, our main way of assessing Proposition 3 is to compare Farr's class with Mayes's and McCartney's classes. Although the proportion of Farr's students in subgroups with high Gini coefficients dropped from 83% in the fall to 65% in the spring, this spring level was still high compared with the other classrooms. It was higher than the spring level for Mayes's class (52% in subgroups with high Gini coefficients) and not too far below the spring level for McCartney's class (76% in subgroups with high Gini coefficients).

Moving from workmate cliques to playmate cliques, look at Figure 6.6. This figure shows the proportions of students in fall and spring playmate subgroups with Gini coefficients that were above the grand median for playmate cliques (that is, above 0.25). Note that, although students' playmate cliques could include students who were enrolled in a classroom other than their own, Figure 6.6 aggregates students according to their classrooms.

In considering the spring levels, as well as changes between fall and spring, it becomes apparent that there is a need for explanations that are more complex than the explanation offered by Proposition 2. In viewing the spring levels from left to right along the figure's horizontal axis, one does not see a consistent rising. What are the main differences between Figures 6.5 and 6.6? What additional hypotheses might help explain the observed patterns for playmate cliques?

Figure 6.6. Proportion of students in playmate subgroups with high Gini coefficients (isolates removed)

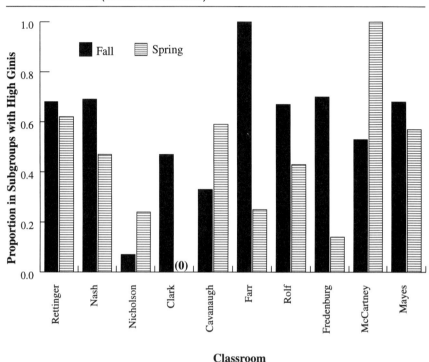

First, students from a few classrooms were situated in dramatically less hierarchical playmate clique structures in the spring than in the fall while their workmate clique structures either became increasingly hierarchical or exhibited only small declines in hierarchy. The classrooms fitting this description are Clark's, Farr's, and Fredenburg's. An examination of the fall and spring playmate cliques for the students from these classrooms suggests that students who were in peripheral positions within hierarchical cliques in the fall shifted their allegiances so that, by spring, they extended their playmate nominations to a different set of students. In general, these students shifted their allegiances to students who reciprocated their nominations more often than their fall nominees had done.

Often the shifting of allegiances involved shifting to students who were not from one's own classroom or shifting to students of the opposite gender. The fact that the shift to dramatically less hierarchical playmate cliques was not accompanied by a shift to dramatically less hierarchical workmate cliques can be explained largely by the fact that students were not able to look to other classrooms for workmate preferences (either in reality or as the question was posed to them). Further, although it was possible to cross lines of gender in one's workmate preferences, this was less common than it was for playmate preferences. A comparison of Tables 6.1 and 6.3 confirms the fact that subgroups that contained both boys and girls were less common among workmate subgroups than they were among playmate subgroups.

Finally, in explaining why the movement toward less hierarchical playmate cliques was not accompanied by a movement toward less hierarchical workmate cliques, it is important to recognize that the workmate nominations had a component of "wish" or "desire" while the playmate nominations primarily reflected actual behaviors. It is easier to maintain an asymmetric, unreciprocated relationship in the realm of wish or desire than it is in the realm of actual behavior. That is, it is easy to want to work with someone even if he or she does not want to work with you, but it is not easy to play with someone who does not play with you.

The main situation in which unreciprocated playmate relationships will be numerous and long-lasting is when play groups are large, as they were for Farr's class in the fall and McCartney's and Mayes's classes in both fall and spring. In this situation, when students are asked to name up to five of their usual playmates (as they were asked in my questionnaire), many of the nominations will be unreciprocated. This is not just an artifact of data collection, however. It is possible in a large playgroup, perhaps a group that regularly plays soccer or tag, for some students to see themselves as being in the game and members of the group while others barely consider these students to be involved. In a small playgroup, however, it is unlikely that a student will see himself or herself as being in the game and a part of the group while others barely recognize his or her presence.

I cannot offer explanations for all of the differences between Figures 6.5 and 6.6; and I cannot offer explanations for all of the ways Figure 6.6 deviates from the predictions of Propositions 2 and 3. But the preceding discussion of Clark's, Farr's, and Fredenburg's classes suggests that some types of relationships (here, usual playmates) are less likely to remain in existence if unreciprocated than are other types of relationships (here, desired workmates). Moreover, the degree of hierarchy characterizing a given network is conditioned by the degree to which individuals have the ability to shift their allegiances in search of a greater likelihood of reciprocation. An individual's ability to shift allegiances in this manner is dependent upon, first, an existent group of others who might reciprocate his or her allegiances and, second, a normative environment that does not proscribe allegiances between the individual and this group of others.

Before ending the discussion of hierarchy versus egalitarianism, I will address the question of whether certain ascriptive traits were associated with centrality within the hierarchical subgroups. Correspondingly, there is the question of whether certain ascriptive traits were associated with peripheral positions within hierarchical subgroups. I found only weak evidence of such associations.

When I examined only the single individual who was most central within each of the hierarchical spring workmate and spring playmate subgroups (those with Gini coefficients above the grand median), there were several settings for which high-SES White students were consistently the most central. Both of the hierarchical spring workmate cliques in Clark's class, the three in McCartney's class, the one in Rettinger's class, and the one in Nicholson's class all had high-SES White students as their most central members. For the other six classrooms, a mixed set of students held the most central positions in the hierarchical workmate subgroups. For hierarchical spring playmate cliques, the two at Fawndale Elementary School and the five at Maple Grove Elementary School all had high-SES White students as their most central members. (More correctly, in one of the hierarchical spring playmate subgroups at Maple Grove, a high-SES White girl from McCartney's class was tied with the sole Asian American girl from McCartney's class as the most central member.)

We can take the previous paragraph's information as moderately strong evidence of a tendency for high-SES White students to hold the most central positions in the hierarchical cliques in some of the settings. Beyond that tendency, however, there was no further association between race/SES and the likelihood of holding a "moderately central" as opposed to "most peripheral" position in hierarchical cliques in any of the settings. Specifically, when I looked beyond the single individual who was most central in each hierarchical clique, it became clear that neither Asian American students nor low-SES non-Asian students were systematically relegated to either the moderately central or the most peripheral positions within these subgroups.

CLOSURE: PATTERNS AND HYPOTHESES

Figure 6.7 shows, for each classroom, the proportion of students (non-isolates) who were in a workmate subgroup with a measure of closure that was above the grand median for workmate cliques. The figure shows both fall and spring levels. The grand median for closure for workmate cliques, based on both fall and spring cliques from all classrooms, was 0.75. This value means that, for a workmate subgroup with the median closure, 75%

Figure 6.7. Proportion of students in workmate subgroups with high closure (isolates removed)

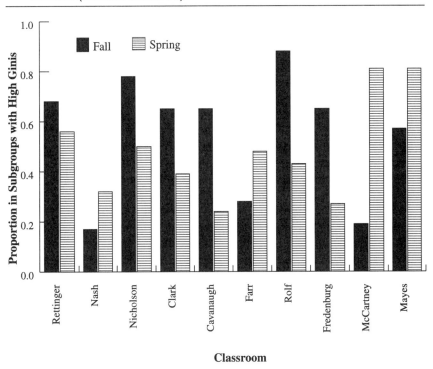

of the workmate nominations extended by the subgroup's members went to other members of the same subgroup.

Figure 6.8 shows the proportion of nonisolates who were in a playmate subgroup with a measure of closure that was above the grand median for playmate cliques. Again, the figure shows both fall and spring levels. The grand median for closure for playmate subgroups was 0.80, just slightly higher than the median for workmate subgroups.

Figures 6.7 and 6.8 reveal that a few classrooms experienced major changes between fall and spring in the proportion of students who were in highly closed subgroups. For workmate subgroups, for example, Cavanaugh's, Rolf's, and Fredenburg's classes all displayed considerable decreases between fall and spring in the proportion of students who were in highly closed cliques. In contrast, McCartney's class displayed a considerable increase between fall and spring.

Figure 6.8. Proportion of students in playmate subgroups with high closure (isolates removed)

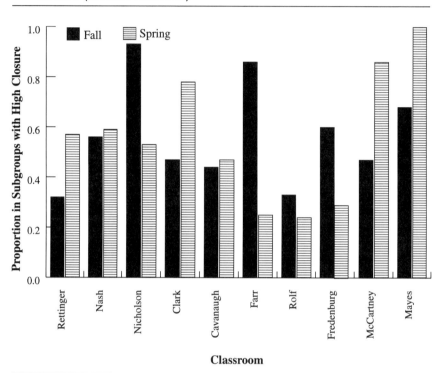

For playmate subgroups, Nicholson's, Farr's, and Fredenburg's classes all experienced considerable decreases between fall and spring in the proportion of students who were in highly closed cliques. In contrast, Clark's, McCartney's, and Mayes's classes all experienced considerable increases between fall and spring.

One thing that is quite apparent about the trends for closure is the way Mayes's and McCartney's classes contrasted with the other eight. These two classrooms that were characterized by strict discipline, high and uniform standards, and a narrow range of topics and performance settings came to display high levels of subgroup closure as the school year progressed. I speculate that the competitive and highly visible environment of these classrooms led students to divide into tight-knit subgroupings. A point to which I will return in Chapter 7 is that the data for Mayes's class suggest that some of the lower achieving students withdrew their ties to some of the class's most vocal academic and social leaders as the year progressed. As they withdrew these ties, they formed anew a couple of fairly closed and cohesive cliques.

Regarding the eight classrooms other than Mayes's and McCartney's, I cannot offer explanations for all of the variation in levels of closure among them. The variation, in itself, is interesting, however. I will draw upon it in Chapter 8 as I discuss the interplay between a classroom's structure and students' participation, perceptions, and attachments.

IN-DEGREE: PATTERNS AND HYPOTHESES

Figure 6.9 shows, for each classroom, the proportion of nonisolates who were in a workmate subgroup with a measure of in-degree that was above the grand median for workmate cliques. This grand median was 0.04, which

Figure 6.9. Proportion of students in workmate subgroups with high in-degree (isolates removed)

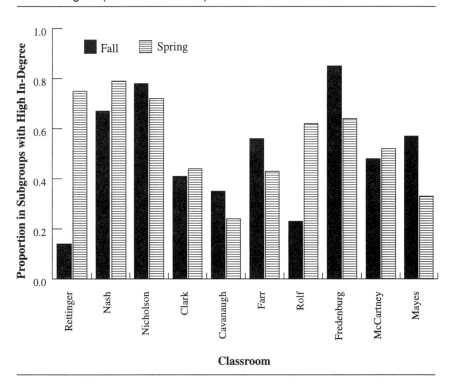

means that a workmate subgroup with the median level of in-degree received, on average, 4% of the nominations extended by the members of each other subgroup in the classroom.

Figure 6.10 shows the proportion of nonisolates who were in a playmate subgroup with a measure of in-degree that was above the grand median for playmate cliques. This grand median was 0.02. This figure may strike the reader as being quite low, but it is consistent with a median closure of 0.80 and a situation in which each school's pair of classrooms was analyzed as a bounded playmate network. Most of these bounded networks contained seven or eight playmate cliques. Given that the distribution of in-degree measures was truncated at the low end, this median of 0.02 makes sense.

One sees by looking at Figures 6.9 and 6.10 that Mayes's and McCartney's classes contrasted with the other eight once again. Especially

Figure 6.10. Proportion of students in playmate subgroups with high in-degree (isolates removed)

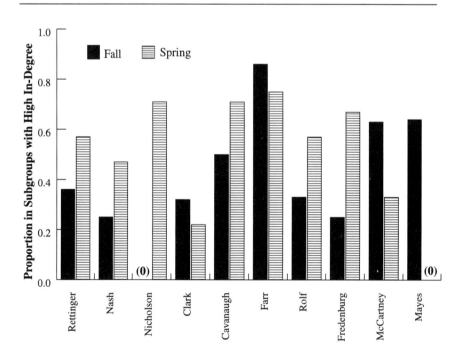

in the trends for playmate subgroups, Mayes's and McCartney's classes displayed considerable decreases in the proportion of students in playmate subgroups with high in-degree. In fact, Mayes's class dropped from having 64% of its students in playmate cliques with high in-degree in the fall to having no students in playmate cliques with high in-degree in the spring.

The other eight classes either experienced more modest decreases in the proportion of students in cliques with high in-degree or experienced increases in this proportion. For some classes (Rettinger's and Rolf's for workmate subgroups, Nicholson's and Fredenburg's for playmate subgroups), these increases were quite large.

Again, I cannot offer explanations for all of the variation in levels of in-degree among these classrooms. The variation is interesting, however, and will be drawn upon in Chapter 8. Furthermore, it will be interesting to consider a classroom's patterns of in-degree in conjunction with its patterns of closure.

To highlight one interesting contrast, consider the closure and in-degree of spring workmate subgroups in Cavanaugh's class and Nash's class, as illustrated in Figures 6.7 and 6.9. Both classes displayed fairly low proportions of students in highly closed subgroups. That is, the majority of students from both classes were in quite open subgroups. The two classes differed, however, in the proportion of students in subgroups with high in-degree. A lot of Nash's students were in subgroups with high in-degree. In fact, three of the four spring workmate subgroups in that class were characterized by high in-degree. This means that the nominations sent between subgroups in this fairly open structure of Nash's were sent to a wide variety of destinations. This suggests a sort of egalitarianism among the subgroups. In contrast, only one of the four spring workmate subgroups in Cavanaugh's class was characterized by high in-degree. Thus, the nominations sent between subgroups in the fairly open structure of Cavanaugh's class were sent predominantly to a single clique. This suggests some hierarchical ordering of the subgroups. Contrasts of the sort seen between Nash's and Cavanaugh's classes will be important in Chapter 8 as we consider the implications of sociometric structure for visibility, normative influence, and reference group processes.

CONCLUSION

This chapter has examined several aspects of the structures and memberships of workmate and playmate subgroups for the 10 classrooms in this study: the salience of ascriptive characteristics, subgroup hierarchy, closure, and in-degree. Regarding ascriptive characteristics, although the classrooms did differ from one another in the extent of homogeneity of workmate and playmate subgroups, no evidence was found to indicate that the salience of students' ascriptive characteristics was related to a classroom's level of personalism and range of performance settings.

Regarding hierarchy within subgroups, the analyses of workmate cliques showed patterns that were fairly consistent with the proposition that a wide range of topics and activities will engender egalitarian structures. This finding for the subgroup level adds to the evidence of Chapter 5, which investigated the distributions of nominations in classrooms considered as wholes. The present chapter's analyses of workmate cliques did not support the third proposition, which hypothesized an interaction between the range of topics and activities, on the one hand, and the rigor and uniformity of academic and disciplinary standards, on the other.

Analyses of playmate cliques suggested that more complex explanations were needed than those used to explain the major trends for workmate cliques. The important points include the fact that an actual playmate relationship is less likely to remain in existence if unreciprocated than is a desired workmate relationship. Further, the degree of hierarchy characterizing subgroup relations is conditioned by the degree to which individuals are free to shift their allegiances in search of a greater likelihood of reciprocation. An individual's ability to shift allegiances in this manner is dependent upon, first, an existent group of others who might reciprocate his or her allegiances and, second, a normative environment that does not proscribe allegiances between the individual and this group of others.

Finally, the analyses of subgroup closure and in-degree suggested that the couple of classrooms characterized by strict discipline, high and uniform standards, and a narrow range of topics and activities stood in sharp contrast to the other eight classrooms because of the extent to which these two classrooms came to be characterized by very closed subgroup structures.

7

A Further Examination of Workmates and Playmates

The analyses of the previous chapters have left unclear the answers to some basic questions about the presence and absence of workmate and playmate nominations. In the analyses of Chapter 6, students who were identified as members of a cohesive subgroup tended to nominate others in the subgroup but, especially in the more hierarchical cliques, some students belonged only because of nominations they extended, not because of nominations they received. Therefore, a classroom might have contained cliques that were internally heterogeneous with respect to race, SES, or gender, while at the same time displaying a low rate of nominations going from the members of one group (e.g., high-SES non-Asian students) to another group (e.g., Asian students).

In this chapter, I examine how frequently workmate and playmate nominations crossed the lines defined by race, SES, and gender. Where dominant patterns are found regarding flows of nominations (e.g., "Nominations sent from Asian students to high-SES non-Asian students were very common, while nominations sent from Asian students to low-SES non-Asian students were very uncommon"), I note classrooms that deviated from these dominant patterns. I ask whether such deviations are explicable in light of what is known about the social organization and context of each school and each classroom.

Where stratification existed along lines of race, SES, or gender, I ask whether this stratification was associated with students' activities and involvements. That is, I ask whether stratification in the flow of nominations was accompanied by stratification in students' activities and involvements. Further, I examine whether the classrooms differed from one another in the likelihood that new workmate and playmate preferences formed during the school year. Where new preferences arose, I investigate whether these were accompanied by students' shared activities and involvements.

THE MODELS

In order to investigate the issues that are outlined above, this chapter presents a set of logistic regression models in which the presence of a spring workmate or playmate nomination between each possible pair of students is predicted. The presence or absence of a nomination from a potential sender to a potential recipient is predicted based upon (1) whether the two students were of the same or different genders; (2) whether they were from the same or different categories defined by race and SES; (3) whether a tie had existed between them in the fall; (4) the number of extracurricular activities they shared; and (5) an interaction term between the presence of a fall tie and the number of shared activities. Additionally, in the case of playmate nominations, whether the two students shared the same teacher is considered. As each of these variables is described in greater detail below, the rationale for including it and the means of interpreting the models' estimated coefficients are discussed.

Unit of Analysis

The unit of analysis in this chapter's models is the unidirectional dyad. In practice, this means that each pair of students is analyzed twice, once to see if "Johnny nominated Xao" and again to see if "Xao nominated Johnny."

The only time a dyad is excluded from the estimation of the models is if the student who was the potential nominator did not participate in the sociometric survey. Even in this situation, however, all dyads in which the nonrespondent was the potential recipient are included in the estimation. For each model of workmate preferences, all possible pairs of students from the classroom under consideration are used in estimating the model. For each model of playmate preferences, all possible pairs of students from the classroom under consideration are used, plus every pair in which a student from the classroom under consideration was the potential recipient and a student from the study's other classroom in that school was the potential nominator.

Independent Variables

For each classroom, a series of three models is estimated for the presence of a spring workmate nomination. The first model ("I") in the series has an intercept and seven independent variables, which are described below. The second model ("II") adds a single independent variable to the baseline model; the third model ("III") adds one more variable. Similarly, for each classroom, a series of three models is estimated for the presence of a spring playmate nomination. The baseline model ("I") for playmate nominations has an intercept, the same seven independent variables as the workmate baseline, and one additional predictor, which is described below. Again, the second and third models ("II" and "III") each add a single independent variable to the baseline model.

The first independent variable in the models of workmate and playmate nominations considers whether the potential nominator and the potential recipient were of the same or different genders. Research by other scholars (e.g., Cone & Perez, 1986; Hallinan, 1979; Schofield, 1982/1989), as well as the insights into the LaCrosse data provided in Chapter 6, suggests that same-gender friendships and associations are the norm for preadolescents. In the comparison of Nash's and McCartney's classrooms in Chapter 6, the tendency for spring workmate preferences to remain within one's own gender group was especially strong in McCartney's class, but it was also in evidence in Nash's class. Documenting this tendency via the regression models is important. Furthermore, in the search for the influence of other factors on students' preferences, it is crucial to begin by accounting for the tendency for workmate and playmate preferences to remain within one's own gender group, thereby disentangling this tendency from other influences.

The actual variable included in the models is labeled "Different Gender." This dichotomous variable takes the value "1" when the potential nominator and the potential recipient were of different genders; it takes the value "0" when the two were of the same gender. In the estimated models, if the coefficients for this variable are negative and significant, this will indicate that cross-gender preferences were substantially less likely than same-gender preferences, controlling for the composition of students in the classroom or pair of classrooms (in the case of playmate nominations).

The next series of variables indicates whether the potential recipient and nominator were from the same or different categories, as defined by race and SES. With the estimated coefficients for these variables one is able to see whether nominations that extended from one group defined by race and SES to another or nominations that remained within a given group were relatively likely or unlikely. I am interested in whether, within a given classroom, certain flows of nominations were much less likely than other flows, and whether particular classrooms stood out from the others by having especially high or low likelihoods of nominations being extended from one group and to another.

Much of the theory and prior research presented in Chapter 2 would lead one to expect that classrooms offering the greatest acquaintance potential to students in the course of daily tasks and activities and those most genuinely encouraging equal status contact would be the classrooms in which student preferences would be least dependent upon the race and SES of the potential nominator and the potential recipient in a dyad. In particular, in these classrooms one would expect the likelihood of nominations being directed toward Asian American students and toward low-SES non-Asian students to approach the likelihood of nominations being directed toward high-SES non-Asian students.

In contrast, in classrooms engendering less acquaintance potential and less equal status contact, one would expect the likelihood of nominations being directed toward these traditionally lower status groups to lag behind the likelihood of nominations being directed toward high-SES non-Asian students. Of course, if these predictions are not borne out fully, it will be wise to consider other relevant contextual factors for each classroom and to consider possible modifications or qualifications to existing theory rather than dismissing the theory outright.

The actual variables used to indicate race and SES in the models are labeled "*to* Asian *from* Same," "*to* Asian *from* Other," "*to* Low-SES Non-Asian *from* Same," "*to* Low-SES Non-Asian *from* Other," and "*to* High-SES Non-Asian *from* Other." Operationally, this is a series of dichotomous variables used to indicate the race and SES of the potential recipient and nominator. For example, "*to* Asian *from* Same" takes the value "1" when both the potential recipient and nominator were Asian American; it takes the value "0" otherwise. The variable "*to* Asian *from* Other" takes the value "1" when the potential recipient was Asian American while the potential nominator was non-Asian (either low-SES or high-SES); it takes the value "0" otherwise.

When one uses a series of dichotomous indicator variables such as these with regression procedures, it is necessary to designate one of the mutually exclusive and exhaustive categories as the excluded reference category. The decision of which category will serve in this capacity is somewhat arbitrary, but it is common to choose a relatively populous category, into which a fairly large number of the units of analysis fall. In this case, I have designated the category in which the potential recipient and nominator were both high-SES non-Asian students as the reference category. Therefore, if an estimated coefficient for "*to* Asian *from* Other" is negative and significant, the interpretation will be that for that classroom a nomination from a non-Asian student to an Asian student was significantly less likely than was a nomination from one high-SES non-Asian student to another, controlling for the demographic composition of the classroom.

The next variable in the models indicates whether a tie had existed between the two students in the fall. Remember that this chapter's models are predicting whether a nomination was extended in the spring. By explicitly modeling whether a previous tie had existed, one gets insight into how likely new workmate and playmate preferences were to arise during the school year in each classroom, relative to the likelihood of fall preferences continuing in the spring.

The actual variable in the models is labeled "No Tie Present in Fall." It takes the value "1" if no nomination was sent from the potential nominator to the potential recipient in the fall of the school year. The absence of a fall nomination could occur either because one of the two students was not enrolled in the class in the fall, or simply because no tie existed between them. A negative and significant estimated effect for this variable will indicate that a newly formed bond (where no nomination had existed in the fall) was significantly less likely than the continuation of a previously existing bond.

In addition to discovering whether the continuation of preexisting allegiances was the predominant trend in all or some of the LaCrosse classrooms, the estimation of an interaction effect between the absence of a fall tie and mutual participation in one or more extracurricular activities by two students will allow us to address other interesting questions. This interaction term and the questions it allows us to address are described below. First, though, I will describe the main effect to be estimated for shared activities.

The variable labeled "Number of Shared Activities" indicates the number of school-based extracurricular activities that were shared by the potential nominator and recipient. Some of these activities took place during the school day; some took place after school. The common characteristics of all of the activities listed by the students are that (1) they took place at the school and (2) they were activities that the whole class was not required to do, but rather that individual students chose to do. The estimated effect of this variable allows us to assess whether workmate and playmate preferences went hand in hand with shared activities. A positive and significant coefficient would indicate that, with each additional shared activity, the likelihood of a workmate or playmate nomination existing between two students increased.

This variable is added to the baseline estimation in the second model for each classroom. By adding the variable in this fashion, one can examine whether the effect of shared activities mediates effects of variables in the baseline model. For example, if the introduction of this variable causes a substantial change in the estimated effect of "No Tie Present in Fall," this may suggest that any tendency for previously established preferences to continue is partially explained by (1) a tendency for fall workmates and playmates to be concentrated in common activities and (2) an association between shared activities and spring preferences. On the other hand, if the introduction of "Number of Shared Activities" does not affect the coefficient for "No Tie Present in Fall," this will suggest that any tendency for previously established preferences to continue exists independently of any significant association between shared activities and spring preferences.

Finally, in the third estimated model for each classroom, an interaction term labeled "Number of Shared Activities *by* No Tie in Fall" is introduced. The estimated effect of this variable, in conjunction with the two main effects, allows one to assess whether shared extracurricular activities were an avenue toward the development of new workmate and playmate preferences or, alternatively, whether shared activities primarily strengthened and entrenched previously existing preferences. Specifically, a positive coefficient for the interaction term will suggest that shared extracurricular activities were more potent in encouraging new preferences than in reinforcing existing ones. On the other hand, a negative coefficient for the interaction term will suggest that shared extracurricular activities were less potent in encouraging new bonds than in reinforcing old ones.

In addition to the various independent variables just described, the models for playmate preferences also include one predictor that the workmate models do not include. This variable, labeled "Same Teacher," takes the value "1" if the potential nominator and the potential recipient were in the same classroom; it takes the value "0" otherwise. Recall that, for playmate nominations, students were invited to name anyone in the school. The estimated models for playmate nominations are based on all possible dyads from the classroom under consideration, plus all dyads in which a student from the classroom under consideration was the potential recipient and a student from the study's other classroom in that school was the potential nominator. Thus, the estimated effect of "Same Teacher" allows one to see whether playmate preferences for others from a student's own classrooms were significantly more or less likely than preferences for students from the other classroom.

Excluded Variables and Other Notes

The models for some of the classrooms have excluded predictors. In this chapter's tables, these instances are indicated by "– – –" and a footnote. Predictors are excluded when a classroom had no dyads of the type represented by the variable (e.g., no dyads in which both students were low-SES non-Asian). In interpreting the models, excluded predictors simply mean that the data from that particular classroom can tell nothing about the effect of that predictor; that classroom can tell nothing about the likelihood of a tie existing in that type of dyad.

A second note about these models is that some coefficients are indicated in the tables as "$-\infty$." These are cases in which absolutely no ties existed in any of the dyads of the type represented by this particular variable. The logistic regression estimation continues iterating to a point at which all other estimated coefficients are stable but the coefficient for this particular variable continues to get increasingly negative with each iteration, without converging. This symbol, $-\infty$, serves to indicate an infinitely small estimated likelihood of a tie existing. While the estimate is technically not statistically significant (because the standard error grows more quickly than the absolute value of the coefficient does), these coefficients can be considered to be substantively significant as the models are interpreted (see a similar notation and interpretation in Yamaguchi, 1992).

FINDINGS

The estimated models are presented in Tables 7.1 through 7.10. The first five tables show the models for workmate nominations. The next five tables show the models for playmate nominations. In discussing all results, I will consider coefficients marked with one or two asterisks to be significant. Although I would not use the models to generalize to a larger population, the size of the marked coefficients relative to their standard errors indicates that each of the corresponding parameters is important in predicting the presence of a nomination. Also, following the logic of the previous section, I am considering coefficients indicated by $-\infty$ to be significant.

Gender

For the models of workmate and playmate nominations, the effect of "Different Gender" is negative and significant without exception (see, for example, the coefficients -1.39, -1.30, and -1.29 for Nash's class across the first three columns of Table 7.1). This reflects the fact that workmate and playmate preferences that crossed the gender line were rare in all of the classrooms. For a few classrooms, absolutely no spring nominations crossed the line of gender. For workmate nominations, these classrooms were Mayes's and McCartney's (see the entries of $-\infty$ for "Different Gender" in Table 7.4). For playmate nominations, these classrooms were Nash's and Mayes's (see the entries of $-\infty$ for "Different Gender" in Tables 7.6 and 7.9).

I was somewhat surprised by this extreme gender segregation for playmates in Nash's class, based upon my observations of those students. I certainly observed girls and boys from her class playing together on the

Table 7.1. Logistic regression models for presence of Spring workmate nomination in Nash's and Nicholson's classes, with dyad as the unit of analysis

Variables	Nash (n=306)			Nicholson (n=324)		
	I	II	III	I	II	III
Intercept	-0.07	-0.45	-0.85	0.53	0.37	-0.02
Different Gender	-1.39**	-1.30**	-1.29**	-1.88**	-1.92**	-1.92**
to Asian *from* Same	0.69	0.78	0.78	0.74	0.87	0.84
to Asian *from* Other	0.17	0.22	0.20	-1.46*	-1.41*	-1.35*
to Low-SES Non-Asian *from* Same	-1.03	-0.99	-1.10	-∞ᵃ	-∞ᵃ	-∞ᵃ
to Low-SES Non-Asian *from* Other	-0.53	-0.52	-0.60	-1.31	-1.25	-1.26
to High-SES Non-Asian *from* Other	0.11	-0.06	-0.29	-0.63	-0.58	-0.52
No Tie Present in Fall	-2.10**	-2.11**	-1.46**	-2.15***	-2.13**	-1.62**
Number of Shared Activities	---	0.23	0.53*	---	0.15	0.59
# Shared Activities * No Tie in Fall	---	---	-0.42	---	---	-0.66

* Coeff./s.e. > 1.65; ** Coeff./s.e. > 1.96
ᵃ The coefficient asymptotically goes to -∞.

118

Table 7.2. Logistic regression models for presence of Spring workmate nomination in Clark's and Cavanaugh's classes, with dyad as the unit of analysis

Variables	Clark (n=289)			Cavanaugh (n=272)		
	I	II	III	I	II	III
Intercept	1.22**	0.75	0.16	0.25	-0.78	-0.77
Different Gender	-3.59**	-3.62**	-4.18**	-2.42**	-2.74**	-2.74**
to Asian *from* Same	0.79	0.98	0.78	-1.56	-1.07	-1.08
to Asian *from* Other	-1.64	-1.53	-1.59	-1.28*	-0.98	-0.98
to Low-SES Non-Asian *from* Same	---a	---a	---a	0.41	0.26	0.26
to Low-SES Non-Asian *from* Other	-0.42	-0.57	-0.53	-0.70	-0.59	-0.59
to High-SES Non-Asian *from* Other	0.04	0.10	0.05	-0.29	0.02	0.02
No Tie Present in Fall	-2.91**	-2.79**	-2.03**	-1.49**	-1.01*	-1.03
Number of Shared Activities	---	0.38**	1.30*	---	0.28**	0.28
# Shared Activities * No Tie in Fall	---	---	-1.05	---	---	0.01

* Coeff./s.e. > 1.65; ** Coeff./s.e. > 1.96
a Variable has been excluded from estimated model because no dyads of the type described by this variable existed.

119

Table 7.3. Logistic regression models for presence of Spring workmate nomination in Farr's and Fredenburg's classes, with dyad as the unit of analysis

Variables	Farr (n=506)			Fredenburg (n=506)		
	I	II	III	I	II	III
Intercept	-0.13	-0.09	-1.30*	-0.26	-0.04	-0.39
Different Gender	-1.61**	-1.61**	-1.76**	-2.08**	-2.09**	-2.09**
to Asian *from* Same	0.10	0.14	-0.62	1.14*	1.18*	1.21*
to Asian *from* Other	0.46	0.46	0.66	0.20	0.18	0.20
to Low-SES Non-Asian *from* Same	$-\infty^a$	$-\infty^a$	$-\infty^a$	-0.02	-0.13	-0.14
to Low-SES Non-Asian *from* Other	-1.39*	-1.40*	-1.26	-1.34*	-1.39*	-1.39*
to High-SES Non-Asian *from* Other	0.04	0.04	0.17	-0.11	-0.15	-0.12
No Tie Present in Fall	-1.79**	-1.81**	-0.47	-1.69**	-1.72**	-1.30*
Number of Shared Activities	---	-0.03	0.77**	---	-0.14	0.09
# Shared Activities * No Tie in Fall	---	---	-1.05**	---	---	-0.32

* Coeff./s.e. > 1.65; ** Coeff./s.e. > 1.96
^{a} The coefficient asymptotically goes to $-\infty$.

120

Table 7.4. Logistic regression models for presence of Spring workmate nomination in Mayes's and McCartney's classes, with dyad as the unit of analysis

Variables	Mayes (n=504)			McCartney (n=506)		
	I	II	III	I	II	III
Intercept	0.10	-0.57	-0.70	0.04	-0.17	0.42
Different Gender	-∞[a]	-∞[a]	-∞[a]	-∞[a]	-∞[a]	-∞[a]
to Asian *from* Same	-∞[a]	-∞[a]	-∞[a]	--[b]	--[b]	--[b]
to Asian *from* Other	-0.91	-1.07	-1.06	0.70	0.81	0.94
to Low-SES Non-Asian *from* Same	2.36	2.78*	2.72*	-1.47*	-1.53*	-1.32*
to Low-SES Non-Asian *from* Other	0.57	0.63	0.62	-1.53**	-1.48**	-1.45**
to High-SES Non-Asian *from* Other	0.84*	0.82	0.82	0.15	0.16	0.15
No Tie Present in Fall	-2.46**	-2.21**	-2.02**	-1.62**	-1.62**	-2.41**
Number of Shared Activities	---	0.73***	0.87*	---	0.22	-0.49
# Shared Activities * No Tie in Fall	---	---	-0.23	---	---	0.88*

* Coeff./s.e. > 1.65; ** Coeff./s.e. > 1.96
[a] The coefficient asymptotically goes to - ∞.
[b] Variable has been excluded from estimated model because no dyads of the type described by this variable existed.

121

Table 7.5. Logistic regression models for presence of Spring workmate nomination in Rolf's and Rettinger's classes, with dyad as the unit of analysis

Variables	Rolf (n=440)			Rettinger (n=357)		
	I	II	III	I	II	III
Intercept	0.42	0.09	-0.08	-0.31	-1.31*	-3.60**
Different Gender	-1.41**	-1.35**	-1.35**	-2.16**	-2.15**	-2.19**
to Asian *from* Same	1.86	2.19	2.13	0.35	0.81	1.17
to Asian *from* Other	0.12	0.33	0.28	-1.45**	-1.23*	-1.16*
to Low-SES Non-Asian *from* Same	-0.90	-0.68	-0.66	$-\infty^a$	$-\infty^a$	$-\infty^a$
to Low-SES Non-Asian *from* Other	-0.53	-0.57	-0.63	$-\infty^a$	$-\infty^a$	$-\infty^a$
to High-SES Non-Asian *from* Other	-0.31	-0.23	-0.25	-0.50	-0.20	-0.17
No Tie Present in Fall	-2.28**	-2.28**	-2.05**	-0.90	-1.03	1.36
Number of Shared Activities	---	0.43**	0.76	---	0.58**	2.16*
# Shared Activities * No Tie in Fall	---	---	-0.38	---	---	-1.64

* Coeff./s.e. > 1.65; ** Coeff./s.e. > 1.96
[a] The coefficient asymptotically goes to - ∞.

Table 7.6. Logistic regression models for presence of Spring playmate nomination in Nash's and Nicholson's classes, with dyad as the unit of analysis

Variables	Nash (n=648)			Nicholson (n=647)		
	I	II	III	I	II	III
Intercept	-1.26**	-1.47**	-1.80**	0.77	0.35	-0.10
Same Teacher	1.80**	1.65**	1.73**	1.85**	1.97**	1.98**
Different Gender	-∞ᵃ	-∞ᵃ	-∞ᵃ	-2.51**	-2.65**	-2.62**
to Asian *from* Same	-0.39	-0.25	-0.28	1.02**	1.35**	1.30**
to Asian *from* Other	-1.67**	-1.62**	-1.67**	-∞ᵃ	-∞ᵃ	-∞ᵃ
to Low-SES Non-Asian *from* Same	-1.34	-1.21	-1.28	-∞ᵃ	-∞ᵃ	-∞ᵃ
to Low-SES Non-Asian *from* Other	-0.91*	-0.85	-0.91*	-∞ᵃ	-∞ᵃ	-∞ᵃ
to High-SES Non-Asian *from* Other	-1.15*	-1.28*	-1.31*	-1.83**	-1.80**	-1.80**
No Tie Present in Fall	-1.05**	-1.12**	-0.71	-3.07**	-3.05**	-2.54**
Number of Shared Activities	---	0.24*	0.48	---	0.34*	0.84*
# Shared Activities * No Tie in Fall	---	---	-0.31	---	---	-0.58

* Coeff./s.e. > 1.65; ** Coeff./s.e. > 1.96
ᵃ The coefficient asymptotically goes to - ∞.

123

Table 7.7. Logistic regression models for presence of Spring playmate nomination in Clark's and Cavanaugh's classes, with dyad as the unit of analysis

Variables	Clark (n=578)			Cavanaugh (n=544)		
	I	II	III	I	II	III
Intercept	-0.23	-0.61	-1.26	-0.57	-0.96*	-0.38
Same Teacher	2.39**	2.43**	2.34**	1.93**	1.86**	1.93**
Different Gender	-1.78***	-1.76***	-1.90**	-3.99***	-4.06**	-4.17**
to Asian *from* Same	0.84	1.06*	1.16*	-0.38	-0.08	-0.26
to Asian *from* Other	-2.87***	-2.75***	-2.76**	-1.18**	-1.04**	-1.02*
to Low-SES Non-Asian *from* Same	1.93	1.54	1.53	-0.87	-0.92	-1.03
to Low-SES Non-Asian *from* Other	0.08	0.05	0.07	-0.82*	-0.77	-0.75
to High-SES Non-Asian *from* Other	-1.41**	-1.31**	-1.29**	-0.73	-0.60	-0.57
No Tie Present in Fall	-2.80**	-2.77***	-1.97***	-1.77***	-1.58**	-2.30**
Number of Shared Activities	---	0.30**	1.28*	---	0.15	-0.08
# Shared Activities * No Tie in Fall	---	---	-1.05	---	---	0.29

* Coeff./s.e. > 1.65; ** Coeff./s.e. > 1.96

124

Table 7.8. Logistic regression models for presence of Spring playmate nomination in Farr's and Fredenburg's classes, with dyad as the unit of analysis

Variables	Farr (n=990)			Fredenburg (n=990)		
	I	II	III	I	II	III
Intercept	-2.17**	-2.35**	-2.76**	-2.40**	-2.28**	-2.67**
Same Teacher	2.75**	2.61**	2.56**	2.81**	2.86**	2.87**
Different Gender	-2.56**	-2.61**	-2.83**	-1.44**	-1.44**	-1.46**
to Asian *from* Same	0.61	0.13	-0.11	1.39**	1.42**	1.41**
to Asian *from* Other	-0.15	-0.30	-0.32	-0.24	-0.26	-0.27
to Low-SES Non-Asian *from* Same	$-\infty^a$	$-\infty^a$	$-\infty^a$	-0.22	-0.31	-0.29
to Low-SES Non-Asian *from* Other	-2.81**	-2.87**	-2.83**	-0.75	-0.79	-0.82
to High-SES Non-Asian *from* Other	0.08	0.01	0.02	-0.49	-0.52	-0.51
No Tie Present in Fall	-1.71**	-1.67**	-0.98**	-1.74**	-1.77**	-1.32*
Number of Shared Activities	---	0.34**	0.81**	---	-0.11	0.18
# Shared Activities * No Tie in Fall	---	---	-0.67**	---	---	-0.35

* Coeff./s.e. > 1.65; ** Coeff./s.e. > 1.96
[a] The coefficient asymptotically goes to - ∞.

Table 7.9. Logistic regression models for presence of Spring playmate nomination in Mayes's and McCartney's classes, with dyad as the unit of analysis

Variables	Mayes (n=1080)			McCartney (n=1032)		
	I	II	III	I	II	III
Intercept	-1.55**	-2.07**	-2.26**	-2.15**	-2.27**	-1.65**
Same Teacher	3.09**	3.12**	3.13**	2.80**	2.79**	2.82**
Different Gender	$-\infty^a$	$-\infty^a$	$-\infty^a$	$-\infty^a$	$-\infty^a$	-2.76**
to Asian *from* Same	-1.54	-1.60	-1.62	$-\infty^a$	$-\infty^a$	$-\infty^a$
to Asian *from* Other	1.17**	1.01**	1.04**	0.20	0.26	0.23
to Low-SES Non-Asian *from* Same	1.72	1.88	1.87	-1.81**	-1.82**	-1.79**
to Low-SES Non-Asian *from* Other	-0.54	-0.50	-0.50	-0.53	-0.51	-0.57
to High-SES Non-Asian *from* Other	1.01**	0.98**	1.01**	-0.60	-0.57	-0.67*
No Tie Present in Fall	-3.17**	-2.98**	-2.76**	-1.83**	-1.82**	-2.52**
Number of Shared Activities	---	0.56**	0.75*	---	0.13	-0.56
# Shared Activities * No Tie in Fall	---	---	-0.28	---	---	0.78

* Coeff./s.e. > 1.65; ** Coeff./s.e. > 1.96
[a] The coefficient asymptotically goes to $-\infty$.

Table 7.10. Logistic regression models for presence of Spring playmate nomination in Rolf's and Rettinger's classes, with dyad as the unit of analysis

Variables	Rolf (n=877)			Rettinger (n=839)		
	I	II	III	I	II	III
Intercept	-0.28	-0.86	-1.43**	-0.36	-0.70	-1.30*
Same Teacher	1.55**	1.74**	1.81**	1.20**	1.12**	1.21**
Different Gender	-1.96**	-1.91**	-1.89**	-3.26**	-3.18**	-3.21**
to Asian from Same	0.09	0.29	0.25	2.43**	2.59**	2.59**
to Asian from Other	-1.85*	-1.68	-1.77*	-0.34	-0.26	-0.26
to Low-SES Non-Asian from Same	-0.83	-0.65	-0.60	1.34*	1.60**	1.66**
to Low-SES Non-Asian from Other	-1.44**	-1.47**	-1.50**	-1.81*	-1.58	-1.62
to High-SES Non-Asian from Other	-1.64**	-1.56**	-1.54**	0.17	0.28	0.35
No Tie Present in Fall	-2.40**	-2.23**	-1.60**	-2.51**	-2.50**	-1.88**
Number of Shared Activities	---	0.34**	0.83**	---	0.24*	0.64*
# Shared Activities * No Tie in Fall	---	---	-0.67*	---	---	-0.49

* Coeff./s.e. > 1.65; ** Coeff./s.e. > 1.96

127

playground and in the classroom at times during the year. At the time of the spring survey, however, no playmate nominations crossed this gender divide.

For Mayes's and McCartney's classes, I was less surprised by the extreme gender segregation that was revealed in the students' survey responses. As I have described in earlier chapters, the great majority of actions and conversations in Mayes's and McCartney's classes were subject to very public scrutiny. There was a lot of chiding, commenting, and teasing in these classrooms. The subject of boyfriends and girlfriends was just beginning to interest the students in Mayes's and McCartney's classes. This subject was beginning to interest students in several of the other classrooms, as well, but in Mayes's and McCartney's classes the amount of chiding and teasing that accompanied talk of boyfriends and girlfriends was greater than in most of the other classrooms. Thus, while the students in these classrooms may have been developing an increasing interest in classmates of the opposite gender, to admit that fact publicly was something to be avoided.

Race and SES

Examining the estimated coefficients for the variable "*to* Asian *from* Same," one sees positive and significant effects in Fredenburg's class for both workmate and playmate nominations, and in Nicholson's, Clark's, and Rettinger's classes for playmate nominations. These positive and significant effects mean that a tie between two Asian American students was more likely in these classrooms than was a tie between two high-SES non-Asian students (the reference category), taking into account the classroom composition (i.e., the number of dyads of each type).

In contrast to these positive and significant effects, the coefficient for "*to* Asian *from* Same" is indicated as $-\infty$ for workmate nominations in Mayes's class. This estimate is based upon only two Asian American students, however. They were a pair of boys who nominated each other as desired workmates in the fall, but did not nominate one another in the spring. The coefficient for "*to* Asian *from* Same" is also indicated as $-\infty$ for playmate nominations in McCartney's class. This estimate is based on nominations that potentially could have gone from the two Asian American boys in Mayes's class to the sole Asian American student in McCartney's (a girl). Neither tie was observed, which is consistent with the extreme gender segregation discussed above for Mayes's and McCartney's classes.

Now examine the estimated coefficients for the variable "*to* Asian *from* Other." In the models of workmate nominations, there are negative and significant effects for Nicholson's, Cavanaugh's, and Rettinger's classes.

In the models of playmate nominations, there are negative and significant effects for Nash's, Nicholson's, Clark's, Cavanaugh's, and Rolf's classes. There is a positive and significant effect for Mayes's class. (The two boys in Mayes's class, discussed above, were fairly popular among their non-Asian classmates as playmates.)

If one considers the effects of "*to* Asian *from* Same" and "*to* Asian *from* Other" jointly, Nicholson's, Clark's, and Rettinger's classes stand out from the others in that Asian American students were highly likely to nominate one another while they were unlikely to receive nominations from non-Asian students. These findings correspond to what I observed during my visits: These were three classrooms in which the Hmong students and the non-Hmong students seemed to be least likely to interact with one another. The intergroup relations were not characterized by animosity; when Hmong students and non-Hmong students were asked to work together, or found themselves side by side, they got along well. Nevertheless, strong friendships or workmate relationships between Hmong and non-Hmong students were not apparent, as they were in some other classrooms.

The estimated effects of "*to* Low-SES Non-Asian *from* Same" and "*to* Low-SES Non-Asian *from* Other" clearly show the low level of popularity or centrality that characterized low-SES non-Asian students in most of the classrooms. Not only were they unlikely to be nominated by Asian American students and high-SES non-Asian students in many of the classrooms, they were also unlikely to be nominated by other low-SES non-Asian students. For the variable "*to* Low-SES Non-Asian *from* Same," there are negative and significant effects for workmate nominations in Nicholson's, Farr's, McCartney's, and Rettinger's classes. There are negative and significant effects for playmate nominations in Nicholson's, Farr's, and McCartney's classes. Positive and significant effects are seen for this variable in Mayes's class for workmate nominations and in Rettinger's for playmate nominations.

My assessment of the positive effect for workmates in Mayes's class is that, by the end of the year, some low-SES students began to feel intimidated by or uncomfortable with some of the high-SES academic leaders in the classroom. Thus, they turned to one another as desired workmates. My assessment of the positive effect for playmates in Rettinger's class is that many of the students with special needs—most of whom were from low-SES families—were not accepted by their classmates as playmates. Their only viable options for playmates were one another. They did not always appear to be happy to play together; they argued and yelled at one another a lot on the playground. But when asked about their usual playmates, they named one another.

For the variable "*to* Low-SES Non-Asian *from* Other," there are negative and significant effects for workmate nominations in Farr's, Fredenburg's, McCartney's, and Rettinger's classes. There are negative and significant effects for playmate nominations in Nash's, Nicholson's, Cavanaugh's, Farr's, Rolf's, and Rettinger's classes.

An important difference between the situation of Asian American students and low-SES non-Asian students in several of these classrooms is that Asian American students generally had strong friendships and support networks with other Asian American students, even if they were not popular among non-Asian students. In contrast, low-SES non-Asian students were likely to lack strong friendships and support networks with their fellow low-SES non-Asian students, as well as with their other classmates.

The most striking thing about the findings regarding high-SES non-Asian students is the difference between the way they related to their classmates as workmates and the way they related to their classmates as playmates. They were much more frequently nominated by Asian American students and by low-SES non-Asian students as workmates than as playmates. Of course, the wording of the questions was different: Students were asked to name students "with whom they would like to work" (as workmates) and students "with whom they usually played" (as playmates).

It is not clear to me whether Asian American students and low-SES non-Asian students desired to play with their high-SES classmates more frequently than they actually did play with them. If I had asked students whom they would like to play with at recess, would more Asian American students and low-SES non-Asian students have nominated high-SES classmates, as they did when asked whom they would like to work with on a science project? Clearly the wording of the questions affects our interpretation. Desiring to work with a classmate is not as dependent upon reciprocation as is actually playing with a classmate. Had there not been limits on the number and subtlety of questions asked of the students, it would have been very interesting to probe more deeply into differences between patterns of desired relationships and patterns of established relationships.

Absence of a Fall Tie, Shared Activities, and Their Interaction

The estimated effect of the variable "No Tie Present in Fall" is negative and significant almost without exception. This suggests that the continuation of previously established workmate and playmate preferences was the dominant trend in these 10 classrooms, rather than the formation of new preferences during the year. The effect of this variable is significant for all 10 classrooms for Model I of playmate nominations. The effect is significant for nine of the 10 classrooms for Model I of workmate nominations: only for Rettinger's class is the effect insignificant. Recall that Rettinger's class, like Rolf's, experienced a major movement of students in the late fall (after the fall data collection) as some students were moved to a third classroom at Riverside Elementary School to ease overcrowded classrooms. Thus, considering this exodus of students, it makes sense that more new workmate relationships would have arisen in Rettinger's classroom than in many of the others.

Not only is the effect of "No Tie Present in Fall" significant in Model I for both workmate and playmate nominations in most classrooms, but the effect remains quite stable with the introduction of "Number of Shared Activities" in Model II with only one noteworthy exception. Where the effect is stable across Models I and II, one can infer that the tendency for previously established preferences to continue is not explained by (1) a tendency for fall workmates and playmates to be concentrated in common activities and (2) an association between shared activities and spring preferences. Rather, the tendency for previously established preferences to continue exists independently of any significant association between shared activities and spring preferences.

The noteworthy exception, in which the effect of "No Tie Present in Fall" is markedly reduced in Model II, is Cavanaugh's class for workmate nominations (note the reduction of the effect from –1.49 to –1.01 between Models I and II for Cavanaugh's class in Table 7.2). For this classroom, the tendency for previously established preferences to continue is partly explained by a concentration of fall workmates in common activities and an association between shared activities and spring preferences.

Cavanaugh's class joins several others in exhibiting a significant association between the number of shared activities and the presence of spring preferences, but in the other classes this association appears to be independent of the tendency for fall preferences to continue. Indeed, these are the main findings related to the variable "Number of Shared Activities." For five classrooms (Clark's, Cavanaugh's, Mayes's, Rolf's, and Rettinger's), the effect of "Number of Shared Activities" is positive and significant in predicting workmate nominations when it is introduced in Model II. For a partially overlapping set of classrooms (Nash's, Nicholson's, Clark's, Farr's, Mayes's, Rolf's, and Rettinger's), the effect of shared activities is positive and significant in predicting playmate nominations when it is introduced in Model II.

It is not surprising to find that shared activities are associated with spring workmate and playmate preferences. This finding is surely a combination of selection and influence: Students who were attracted to one another as friends and workmates were likely to join common activities;

and common activities were likely to encourage friendships and workmate preferences.

While selection and influence surely coexist, the introduction of the interaction term, "Number of Shared Activities *by* No Tie in Fall," in Model III allows one to explore some subtleties. Specifically, the introduction of the interaction term allows one to assess whether shared activities were an avenue toward the development of new workmate and playmate preferences in these classrooms or, alternatively, whether shared activities primarily strengthened and entrenched previously existing preferences. Note that, although the continuation of previously existing preferences was the dominant trend in these classrooms, some new preferences did arise. An interesting question is whether these somewhat rare new preferences were especially likely to arise in conjunction with shared activities.

The interaction term is not significant for very many of the classrooms but, in light of the cases in which it is significant, interesting interpretations are suggested. The only occurrence of a positive and significant interaction term is for the model of workmate nominations for McCartney's class (see the coefficient 0.88 in the last column of Table 7.4). This positive effect suggests that shared activities sparked new preferences in McCartney's class.

Recall that McCartney's class was characterized by strict discipline and a narrow range of topics and performance settings. On a typical day, opportunities for informal mixing and contact between students were much more constrained in McCartney's classroom than in many of the other classrooms.

An intriguing possible interpretation of the positive effect found for McCartney's classroom is that her students latched onto extracurricular activities as a rare opportunity to meet and interact with classmates whom they would not otherwise get to know intimately. In other classrooms, opportunities to meet and interact with a wide range of classmates in a personalistic manner were less rare, so that extracurricular activities might not have stood out as such unique contexts and, thus, the interaction term is not seen to be significant.

The other models in which the estimated effect of the interaction term is positive, although not significant, are for Cavanaugh's class for both workmate and playmate nominations and, again, for McCartney's class—this time for playmate nominations. The second occurrence of a positive (albeit insignificant) coefficient for McCartney's class adds credence to the interpretation given above. As for Cavanaugh's class, a somewhat similar interpretation can be given. Recall that Cavanaugh's class displayed high levels of student mobility, with students moving both in and out of the school during the year. The combination of high rates of movement both into and out of Cavanaugh's class differentiated it from other classrooms, like Rolf's and Rettinger's, in which movement out of the classroom was the main component of student mobility. I stated in Chapter 4 that the combination of in-migration and out-migration presented Mrs. Cavanaugh with challenges in building cohesion among students. Just as extracurricular activities may have functioned in McCartney's class as an otherwise rare context for students to interact and form new bonds, they may have functioned in Cavanaugh's class to satisfy a strong demand for otherwise unacquainted students to meet one another and to form new bonds.

The interaction term is negative and significant in three instances—for Farr's class for models of both workmate and playmate nominations, and for Rolf's class for the model of playmate nominations. I do not have a ready explanation for the negative coefficient for the model of playmate nominations for Rolf's class. For Farr's class, however, the negative coefficients are consistent with the ambivalence I perceived among many of the parents and students who were new to Fawndale Elementary School in the wake of the busing plan regarding how much time and energy they would invest in the school and their children's new classmates (see Chapter 3). It is consistent with what I observed in Farr's classroom, and at Fawndale generally, to speculate that many of the students who were new to the school were somewhat resistant to forming new bonds with some of their classmates. The data suggest that many of the students who were new to Fawndale were highly likely to retain their strongest allegiances to old friends and that this likelihood became even greater as they shared activities with their new schoolmates. Furthermore, some of the students who had been at Fawndale prior to the busing plan were highly likely to retain their strongest allegiances to old friends and, again, this likelihood became even greater as they shared activities with their new schoolmates. From the present analyses, one cannot tell whether the students who had been at Fawndale prior to the busing formed their preferences before, simultaneously with, or in reaction to their new classmates' preferences. Any one of these scenarios, however, has interesting implications.

The revised contact hypothesis of Chapter 2 offers one possible explanation of social relations in Farr's class. This hypothesis stresses the necessity of contact under equal-status conditions in order for positive affect and interaction to result as previously separated groups come together. While Mrs. Farr was as conscientious and proactive as any of the 10 teachers about providing a classroom environment that offered opportunities for success and high status to all students, it may have been that the highly public and emotional nature of the busing plan as it affected Fawndale Elementary School still precluded true equal-status contact in the second year of the plan. Thus, although new schoolmates were coming together in common activities, the contact in these activities may not have been of a sort that would spark new workmate and playmate relationships.

CONCLUSION

In this chapter I have examined how frequently spring workmate and playmate nominations crossed the lines defined by race, SES, and gender in the 10 classrooms. Further, I have examined the likelihood that new workmate and playmate preferences formed between fall and spring, as opposed to the continuation of fall preferences. Finally, I have investigated the relationship between students' shared extracurricular activities and students' workmate and playmate preferences. As a part of this investigation of extracurricular activities, I have asked whether shared activities played a special function in either sparking new workmate and playmate relationships or, alternatively, strengthening and entrenching previously existing preferences.

The results certainly did not reveal a simple story by which the classrooms that seemed to offer the greatest acquaintance potential and most genuinely to encourage equal-status contact—classrooms like Rettinger's, Nash's, Nicholson's, Clark's, and Cavanaugh's—contained flows of workmate and playmate nominations that were largely independent of race and SES. Indeed, Rettinger's, Nicholson's, and Clark's classes stood out from others in the fact that their Asian American students were highly likely to nominate one another while they were relatively unlikely to receive nominations from non-Asian students. Many questions remain about the factors that guided peer relations in these classrooms. Some of these questions, and future research designs that might better answer them, will be articulated in Chapter 9. First, though, the present chapter has pointed out the need to pay careful attention to at least two important and intertwined themes that seem to be crucial to any adequate explanation of patterns of peer relations.

The first of these themes might be called an ecological theme. This theme was present in the intriguing possible explanations of the positive interaction terms involving the absence of fall ties and shared activities in the models for McCartney's and Cavanaugh's classes. The suggestion was that, over and above the dominant trends and patterns that seem to have influenced all of the classrooms, opportunities such as extracurricular activities functioned differently depending on the specific offerings and environment of a classroom. Where strict discipline and a narrow range of topics and performance settings limited the opportunities McCartney's students had to interact informally and personalistically, it may have been that extracurricular activities fulfilled an otherwise unmet demand. Similarly, where high levels of student mobility made it difficult for Cavanaugh's students to meet one another and form new bonds, extracurricular activities may have functioned to satisfy a demand that was unique (at least in its strength) in that classroom.

The second theme relates to student mobility, students' enrollment histories, and the particulars of the desegregation plan. Many of the explanations offered in this chapter hinged upon an understanding of movement into and out of classrooms or schools. This second theme was present in the discussion of Cavanaugh's classroom in tandem with the ecological theme; hence I say the two themes are intertwined. This second theme was also present in the discussions of Rettinger's class and Farr's class.

Chapter 8 will retain an awareness of the ecological conditions of each classroom and the ways students' enrollment histories may have affected their roles and structural positions in their classrooms. With these themes in mind, as well as the related issue of task and reward structures, I move now to the consideration of students' feelings of belonging and their participation in classroom life.

8

The Roots
of Belonging
and Participation

In this chapter, I want to suggest some of the ways in which classroom organization and the structure of peer relations affect an individual's feelings of belonging and participation in classroom activities. This chapter is, in a sense, a statement of some of the reasons why the findings of Chapters 5, 6, and 7 are important. In the previous chapters I have argued that the combination of a classroom's task and reward structure and the conditions under which its students come to be there (for the present study, students' enrollment histories before and after the desegregation plan) have considerable influence over patterns of peer relations. In this chapter, I contend that those three components—task and reward structure, the conditions which bring students together, and the structure of peer relations—have strong influence on the degree to which each student defines himself or herself, and is defined by others, as belonging to the group. The three components shape each student's conception of his or her place, and the places of others, within the classroom. Further, these components largely determine rates and types of participation in classroom activities.

In order to develop this argument, I begin this chapter by considering in greater depth some structural characteristics of peer relations and their likely effects on feelings of belonging and participation. Specifically, I return to three of the traits of cohesive subgroups that were introduced in Chapter 6. These were the degree of hierarchy, closure, and in-degree.

After I develop some theories about how the structural characteristics of a subgroup may affect individuals within that subgroup, the chapter continues with portrayals of three pairs of students. For these pairs, I will draw upon the tasks and rewards of their classrooms, the circumstances that brought the students together with their classmates, and the structure of peer relations in discussing the types of classroom participation in which I witnessed each student being engaged.

Each pair of students is interesting because its two students had some things in common in the fall of the year but, by the spring, differed from one another in important ways. Thus, the style of argument will be similar to that used to compare Nash's class with McCartney's in Chapter 6. Finally, this chapter concludes with some discussion about the relationship between task and reward structures and the emergence of reference groups, as well as the subsequent implications of reference groups for students' participation and feelings of belonging.

LOCATION, LOCATION, LOCATION

Recall that Chapter 6 considered the proportion of each classroom's students who were located within subgroups characterized by high or low levels of hierarchy, closure, and in-degree. A subgroup's degree of hierarchy was measured by a Gini coefficient, and represented the extent to which workmate or playmate nominations extended within the subgroup were evenly distributed among its members. Closure was defined as the proportion of all nominations extended by a subgroup's members that remained within the subgroup. Finally, in-degree was measured as the proportion of other cliques' nominations that were received by the members of the subgroup in question.

If one draws upon the dichotomies of high versus low levels once again, and then cross-classifies by the three dichotomies, one derives the very useful eight-celled framework depicted in Figure 8.1. The eight cells constitute mutually exclusive and exhaustive structural locations for students and their subgroups. I contend that each of the eight locations has a distinct set of properties that has implications for a student's feelings of belonging and participation. (The figure's indication of structural locations for students named Kim and Amy will be referenced later in this chapter.)

A student's location within the classroom's social structure conditions the frequency and quality of interactions with classmates. This location is the vantage point from which he or she observes and assesses classmates; it is also the position in which he or she is viewed and assessed by classmates.

Because cohesive subgroups, like those considered in Chapter 6, are very real and salient features of classrooms, one can gain much understanding from considering the structural attributes of a student's subgroup, as well as the student's position within the subgroup. If one considers these factors in conjunction with the broader pattern of social relations (i.e., the structural attributes of other subgroups in the classroom), one has a very informative portrait of the vantage point from which the student sees and

Figure 8.1. Categorization of subgroups by degree of hierarchy, in-degree, and closure

Degree of Hierarchy: Low

	IN-DEGREE *Low*	IN-DEGREE *High*
CLOSURE *Low*	*a*	*b* Kim, Spring, work
CLOSURE *High*	*c* Kim, Fall, play	*d* Amy, Fall, work

Degree of Hierarchy: High

	IN-DEGREE *Low*	IN-DEGREE *High*
CLOSURE *Low*	*e*	*f* Kim, Fall, work
CLOSURE *High*	*g* Amy, Spring, work Amy, Spring, play	*h* Amy, Fall, play Kim, Spring, play

experiences, and the position in which the student is seen and experienced by others.

The categorization of subgroups by degree of hierarchy, closure, and in-degree presented in Figure 8.1 allows one to consider several contrasting structural locations, and the implications of these locations for belonging and participation. First, consider the ramifications of a subgroup's being on one side or the other of the dichotomy of each of the three constructs.

Specifically, consider the dynamics of a subgroup with high closure (cells *c*, *d*, *g*, and *h*). The members of such a subgroup have their attention and allegiance turned very much inward toward one another. A student in such a subgroup probably draws attitudinal and behavioral cues almost exclusively from the other members of the subgroup. His or her primary feelings of belonging would be attached to the subgroup, rather than to the larger class. To the extent that members of a closed subgroup react to other subgroups, these are probably reactions of opposition and contrast. That is, if students from a closed subgroup define themselves in relation to students from another subgroup, it is likely by way of focusing on the differences between the two subgroups.

In contrast, consider the dynamics of a subgroup with low closure (cells *a*, *b*, *e*, and *f*). The interpersonal relations and perceptions of a student in such a subgroup could be very different from those of a student in a closed subgroup. Subgroups with low closure are characterized by numerous allegiances that go to other subgroups. A student in this setting would probably direct his or her feelings of belonging to the entity of the whole class at least as much as to the more proximate subgroup. Attitudinal and behavioral cues would be taken from a relatively wide range of classmates.

In-degree is, of course, sort of the flip side of closure. Whereas closure is measured according to the allegiances that are extended *by* members of a subgroup across subgroup boundaries, in-degree is measured according to the allegiances that are extended *to* members of a subgroup across subgroup boundaries. Thus, the main differences associated with being in a subgroup with high in-degree (cells *b*, *d*, *f*, and *h*) as opposed to low in-degree (cells *a*, *c*, *e*, and *g*) involve an individual's perception of how much affect, deference, and attention that student and his or her most proximate peers receive from other members of the class. Being a member of a subgroup with high in-degree probably makes a student perceive a position of leadership and prestige within the larger class. In contrast, being a member of a subgroup with low in-degree probably makes the student perceive that his or her actions and attitudes are primarily relevant to those within the most proximate circle of peers.

The implications of being in a subgroup with a high degree of hierarchy (cells *e*, *f*, *g*, and *h*) depend upon whether the student is central, peripheral, or in a more moderate position within the hierarchy. The activities, attitudes, and identity of a hierarchical subgroup are strongly driven by its most central members. The central members wield disproportionately strong influence in establishing norms and standards. Peripheral members probably place a lot of stock in the attitudes and behaviors of their more central friends. This deference, or placing of stock, would generally not be reciprocated.

In contrast, all members of a subgroup with a low degree of hierarchy (cells *a*, *b*, *c*, and *d*) probably contribute fairly equally in establishing the activities, attitudes, and identity of the subgroup. There would typically be a lot of mutual dependence and reciprocation as individuals assessed themselves relative to one another.

Beyond the implications of a student's subgroup being located on one side or the other of the dichotomy of each of the three constructs, additional nuances emerge when multiple dichotomies are considered simultaneously. That is, each of the eight cells in Figure 8.1 has unique characteristics determined by the intersection of hierarchy, closure, and in-degree.

For example, the experience of being a member of a subgroup with high closure is different depending upon whether the subgroup is characterized by high or low in-degree. In the case of high closure coupled with high in-degree (cells *d* and *h*), the subgroup member probably perceives that he or she holds an exclusive and highly admired position within the class. The individual and his or her peers are not extending many allegiances or much deference to other cliques within the class, but they are receiving these from other cliques. In the case of high closure coupled with low in-degree (cells *c* and *g*), the subgroup member probably is aware that his or her most proximate circle of peers proceeds through daily life at a considerable social distance from most of their classmates.

Continuing, for these two different types of subgroups, there are added subtleties that come with being either (1) central in a hierarchical subgroup, (2) peripheral in a hierarchical subgroup, or (3) embedded in an egalitarian subgroup. These three conditions impact the degree to which the individual looks to others, or is looked to by others, for behavioral and attitudinal cues.

It would require a separate book in itself to discuss all of the subtleties that make each of the eight cells unique. Furthermore, this is not the place to explore every aspect of the interplay between an individual's subgroup being located in any particular cell within the framework and the variety of possible arrangements for other subgroups within the framework. Although I cannot accomplish those things fully here, nevertheless, this initial description of how a subgroup's degree of hierarchy, closure, and in-degree can impact an individual's feelings of attachment and participation can be useful in the consideration of three pairs of students from the LaCrosse classrooms.

FOCUSING ON STUDENTS

Kim and Amy

The first pair of students I want to present are Kim and Amy. Both were White girls from high-SES families. Kim was enrolled in Mrs. Nash's class at New Forest Elementary School, and Amy was enrolled in Mrs. McCartney's class at Maple Grove Elementary School.

Regarding patterns of peer relations in these two classrooms, recall from Chapter 6 that Nash's class declined somewhat between fall and spring in the proportion of students who were in highly hierarchical workmate subgroups (from 61% to 42% in subgroups with Gini coefficients above the grand median). Further, Nash's class increased slightly between fall and spring, but remained at a fairly low level, in the proportion of students who were in highly closed workmate subgroups (from 17% to 32%). The class rose between fall and spring and ended at a fairly high level in the proportion of students who were in workmate subgroups with high in-degree (from 67% to 79%).

In Nash's class, the changes in the structure of playmate cliques were similar to the changes for workmate cliques. The proportion of students in very hierarchical playmate subgroups dropped considerably between fall and spring; the proportion in highly closed playmate subgroups rose slightly between fall and spring; and the proportion of students in playmate subgroups with high in-degree rose considerably between fall and spring.

In McCartney's class, changes in the patterns of peer relations were very different from the changes in Nash's class, as Chapter 6 illustrated. McCartney's class increased between fall and spring in the proportion of students in highly hierarchical workmate subgroups (from 48% to 76%). Further, McCartney's class increased by a large amount in the proportion of students in highly closed workmate subgroups (from 19% to 81%). The class rose only slightly between fall and spring in the proportion of students who were in workmate subgroups with high in-degree (from 48% to 52%). The changes in the structure of playmate subgroups were similar to the changes in workmate subgroups in McCartney's class, except that the proportion of students in playmate subgroups with high in-degree declined rather than increased.

In selecting Kim and Amy as two students to be compared, I have chosen students whose changing subgroup settings closely mirrored the changes that took place in their respective classrooms. To aid us in characterizing each student's subgroup setting, the placements of the two girls' fall and spring subgroups within the eight-celled framework are indicated in the appropriate cells of Figure 8.1. Also, further understanding of the structural locations of these two girls in relation to their classmates can be gained by looking back to the sociograms of Figures 6.1–6.4. In Figures 6.1 and 6.2, Kim is represented as student #8. In Figures 6.3 and 6.4, Amy is represented as student #106.

Kim's fall workmate subgroup was situated in cell f, characterized by a high degree of hierarchy, low closure, and high in-degree. Kim was the most central member of this subgroup. In the spring, Kim's workmate subgroup was located in cell b, characterized by a low degree of hierarchy, low closure, and high in-degree. The main change in Kim's workmate setting, then, was a shift toward more egalitarian relations while she remained in a subgroup setting with fairly permeable boundaries, as evidenced by both low closure and high in-degree.

Kim's fall playmate subgroup was situated in cell c, and her spring playmate subgroup was situated in cell h. So, in her playmate relations, Kim's setting became increasingly hierarchical, while receptiveness toward members of other subgroups remained low (as evidenced by high closure in both fall and spring) and popularity among members of other subgroups increased (as evidenced by increased in-degree).

Amy's fall workmate subgroup was situated in cell d, characterized by a low degree of hierarchy, high closure, and high in-degree. In the spring, Amy's subgroup was located in cell g, characterized by a high degree of hierarchy, high closure, and low in-degree. Amy was the most central member of this subgroup. The main changes in Amy's workmate setting between fall and spring were a shift toward more hierarchical relations and a shift toward less popularity among members of other subgroups, while receptiveness toward members of other subgroups remained low.

Amy's fall playmate subgroup was situated in cell h, and her spring playmate subgroup was in cell g. In both fall and spring, she shared with others the claim of being the most central member of her playmate subgroup. The main change in her playmate setting, then, was a shift toward less popularity among members of other subgroups, while the degree of hierarchy remained high and receptiveness toward members of other subgroups remained low.

How did Kim's and Amy's subgroup settings, and the shifts between fall and spring, relate to their patterns of participation in the classroom? First, Kim appeared to relate to a larger number of the students in her class than Amy did as the school year progressed. I would attribute this contrast largely to the contrast between (1) the tendency toward a low degree of hierarchy, low degree of closure, and high in-degree that characterized Kim's workmate subgroup setting, as well as the workmate and playmate subgroup settings of most of her classmates, and (2) the tendency toward a high degree of hierarchy, high degree of closure, and fairly low in-degree that characterized Amy's workmate and playmate subgroup settings, as well as the workmate and playmate settings of most of Amy's classmates. Kim's playmate subgroup setting is not consistent with my explanation, but I would argue that playmate relations are secondary to workmate relations in explaining how students interact and participate within the classroom.

As evidence that Kim related, as a workmate and as a friend, to a larger number of students in her class than Amy did, I can cite the large number of times that Kim was involved in conversations or interactions with students who were in neither her workmate nor her playmate subgroups, but who were students with whom she was friendly and comfortable. For example, every day the class had 15–20 minutes to read silently immediately after lunch and recess. During this reading time, students could either remain at their desks or move anywhere else in the room. On the first day of school, seven of the girls in the class, including Kim, chose to sit together on the windowsill as they read. The next day a somewhat different set of students—two boys and five girls, including Kim—sat together on the windowsill during reading time. On the third day, Kim joined yet another set of four other girls on the floor to read. This pattern of an absence of rigid cliques was established early in the year in Nash's class and continued throughout the year.

On the first day of my spring visit to Nash's class, Kim was absent. When she returned the next day, I said, "hello," and told her that I was visiting the class as I had in the fall and the winter. Jordan, a boy in the class, was eager to explain to me that Kim had been in Washington, D.C., and Milwaukee with her family. In a small way, Jordan's knowing and sharing where Kim had been during her absence reflected the extent to which all of Nash's students knew and cared about one another's activities and home lives.

The main way I can contrast Amy with Kim in terms of the number of classmates with whom each girl regularly related as a workmate and a friend is by citing for Amy an absence of instances like those I have described for Kim. There were a large number of students to whom I never saw Amy speak and, in general, Amy's interactions were more heavily concentrated with a small group of friends than Kim's were.

The fact that Kim related to a larger number of her classmates as a workmate and as a friend than Amy did draws attention to a resource that Mrs. Nash had at her disposal during the school year in greater abundance than Mrs. McCartney did. This resource was students' receptiveness toward working with one another in almost any groupings or pairings. At numerous times during my observations of McCartney's class, students were asked to work on assignments with the others at their desk clusters. Generally these were clusters of four or five desks; at most times during the year they were groupings that Mrs. McCartney had assigned with the intention of mixing students with respect to gender and ability level. It was quite common for all of the students at a desk cluster to ignore Mrs. McCartney's request; each student would open his or her book and work independently, neither solving problems in cooperation with the others nor comparing answers with the others. It also happened several times that most of the students at a desk cluster would want to work cooperatively, as Mrs. McCartney had instructed, but that one or two students would refuse to work with the others. In these cases, the group of students who wanted to work cooperatively would either call to Mrs. McCartney and tell her that their deskmates were not cooperating, or those who wanted to work cooperatively would do so, ignoring the students who refused to join.

In Nash's class, in contrast, students worked cooperatively and with enthusiasm in almost any groupings. If anything, Mrs. Nash had the problem that her students were too friendly and familiar with one another and wanted to joke and play more than they wanted to work. But it was clear that they were receptive to almost any pairings or groupings, and to groupings that changed frequently.

One thing that Nash's students disliked were permanent groupings that branded them as high or low achievers. When I asked Mrs. Nash whether she ever used ability grouping in her classroom, she said that, as a rule, she did not, but that on any given day she might ask a group of students who were all having trouble with the same skill or topic to work together. Part of her reason for assembling these temporary groupings was so that she could give them special instruction. She said that early in the year students had disliked this practice very much. She told them that they would be working together only for the day, not permanently. The students were still unhappy until the next day when they could see, in fact, that the groupings were not permanent. After some time, the students came to trust fully that groupings like these were for single days only; then they would work in them willingly.

Finally, to return more specifically to my observations of Amy and Kim, I will describe Amy's reaction during the time when a substitute teacher was instructing McCartney's class. As described in Chapter 4, Mrs. McCartney was absent for about 6 weeks in January and February. My fall and spring visits to the classroom were at times when Mrs. McCartney was teaching. My winter visit was at a time when the substitute was teaching. The contrast in Amy's attitudes and participation in the winter, as compared to the fall and spring, was striking. In the fall and spring, Amy almost always was one of the first students to raise a hand and to volunteer to answer questions. She regularly received a lot of praise from Mrs. McCartney for her academic work, more than most other students received.

Although, in Figure 4.3, I characterized Mrs. McCartney as having very uniform disciplinary standards, she seemed to allow some extra playfulness from Amy. Amy had a twin sister in Mayes's classroom. As mentioned in Chapter 4, a movable partition separated Mayes's room from McCartney's room. When the partition was removed, Amy and her sister would often smile, wave, or send hand signals to each other. When the partition was mostly closed, but with a small opening, Amy or her sister would sometimes look into the other classroom and try to get the other's attention. On one occasion, Amy's sister stood grinning and whispering at the partition as Mrs. McCartney taught. Mrs. McCartney and Amy looked up and saw her at the same time. With an amused look on her face, Mrs. McCartney told Amy to ignore her sister as the lesson continued. Many minor instances like this one revealed the playful and lenient relationship between Amy and Mrs. McCartney.

When the substitute teacher was leading the class, however, Amy's eagerness to participate and her cheerful playfulness disappeared almost completely. She almost never volunteered an answer when the substitute was teaching. One day when I was observing in Mayes's class, Amy came to the partition, almost in tears, and told her sister that the substitute teacher had not liked the story she had written and wanted her to rewrite it. On this day, and throughout the time I saw Amy during my winter visit to Maple Grove, she looked unhappy and withdrawn.

The point I draw from the change in Amy's attitudes and participation is that students who are most central in hierarchically structured classrooms derive much of their status and prestige from the activity and reward structure presented by the teacher. When the substitute teacher did not offer Amy the rewards to which she was accustomed—either the praise for her academic work or amused tolerance of her playful antics—she enjoyed school much less than usual and participated in classroom activities much less than usual.

Tong and Lor

The second pair of students to be discussed are Tong and Lor. Both were Hmong boys from low-SES families. Tong was enrolled in Mrs. Farr's class at Fawndale Elementary School, and Lor was enrolled in Mrs. Cavanaugh's class at Campus Edge Elementary School. A main point that I want to communicate as I discuss Tong and Lor is that there is a crucial interplay between (1) the set of roles inherent in a classroom's task, reward, and prestige structures and (2) the personality and predispositions of each student. This crucial interplay affects each student's satisfaction, eagerness to participate, and (at times) ability to participate in classroom activities.

In considering Tong and Lor, I will not delve into their subgroups' positions in the framework of Figure 8.1 as deeply as I did for Kim and Amy; the two boys did not diverge from one another in terms of their positions in the eight-celled framework as dramatically as Kim and Amy did. A brief overview will suffice. Tong moved from a fall workmate subgroup in cell *e* to a spring workmate subgroup in cell *h*; he moved from a fall playmate clique in cell *h* to a spring playmate clique in cell *b*. Lor's fall workmate subgroup was in cell *e*, and his fall workmate subgroup was in cell *f*; his fall playmate subgroup was in cell *c*, and his spring playmate subgroup was in cell *h*. By the spring, each boy came to be more tightly linked to some of the White boys in his class than he had been in the fall. Lor shared claim to being the most central member of his fairly hierarchical spring play clique but was much less central within his fairly hierarchical spring work clique. In contrast, Tong was quite central within his spring work clique and joined others in a fairly egalitarian (low hierarchy) spring play clique.

Tong and Lor were quite different from one another in the ways they participated and related to their classmates as the school year progressed. Tong emerged as a very outgoing and popular member of Farr's class. He was a big, athletic boy; among a group of boys (and one girl) who were very competitive in the football and basketball games they played at recess, Tong was respected and liked. He was confident and eager in giving answers in class, although he was by no means the top academic performer in the classroom. But his confidence and eagerness afforded him considerable status in a classroom with high and uniform academic standards.

My impression is that Tong gained status and popularity because he competed well athletically and academically in a setting where those things were valued highly. I cannot understate the part of his status and popularity that was derived because of his athletic prowess and gregarious nature. During my winter visit, I accompanied Farr's students to music class. The music teacher said that I could sit anywhere I wished. I said that I'd take a seat in the back row. One of the boys in the back row said, "Yeah, with the big guys." The students in this back row were, indeed, the biggest students in the class; they were two White boys, Tong, and Christine, a strong and athletic girl who regularly played football with the boys.

One of Tong's friends and classmates was Houa, the other Hmong boy in Farr's class. Although he was probably a better student than Tong, Houa was much shier and more reserved and considerably less athletic. He received fewer workmate and playmate nominations than Tong in both fall and spring. The fact that Houa received fewer workmate nominations than Tong shows that academic prowess alone did not make one a desired workmate in Farr's class. At least among the boys in Farr's class, one also had to be somewhat gregarious and competitive in order to be highly popular as a workmate.

A contrast to Tong's situation in Farr's class exists in the ways Lor participated and related to his classmates in Cavanaugh's class. Like Tong, Lor had an outgoing and jovial personality. He was a popular playmate and was competitive in the games played at recess and in gym class. In the regular classroom, however, Lor's role was different. Whereas Tong's manner of relating to his classmates as a good-natured and able competitor spanned both the playground and the classroom, Lor's time in the classroom often found him placed in the role of a student who was to receive academic help. It was clear to me that Cavanaugh's class was one in which students were encouraged to help one another with their school work. Some students consistently received praise for helping others. Some other students consistently seemed to enjoy receiving help from others. Lor, however, fell into neither of these groups and often seemed to resist the role of "the one who needed help."

His attitudes and participation in class seemed to vary according to whether or not he felt threatened and insulted by being placed in the role of the one who needed help. During much of the year, Mrs. Cavanaugh had Lor paired with Eric, a high-SES White classmate, when students worked together for math and other academic subjects. Eric and Lor had a relationship that was difficult for me to understand initially. At the time of my fall visit to Cavanaugh's classroom, I noted that when Mrs. Cavanaugh asked the two boys to work together for math, both boys made angry faces and did not appear to want to work together. Ten minutes later, when it was time for a snack break, Lor walked to Eric's desk, and they shared some food and talked happily.

On the first day of my winter visit to Cavanaugh's class, Lor sat down next to Eric at the beginning of the time allotted for math work. Lor said to Eric, "I'm your partner, remember?" Eric responded, somewhat sarcastically, "How could I forget?" The two boys worked together that day, but without a high level of communication between them.

On the following day, they were not working together during math although Mrs. Cavanaugh had intended that they would. At the beginning of the time allotted for math work, Lor had stood by Eric's desk. They spoke to one another for a few seconds, and then each sat at his own desk and worked alone. After about 12 minutes, Mrs. Cavanaugh asked, "Lor, aren't you and Eric going to work together?" Lor shook his head, indicating "no." Mrs. Cavanaugh looked disappointed and confused for a second and then said, "Well, you two are partners. Are you getting along okay, Lor?" Lor said, "Yes." Mrs. Cavanaugh said nothing else. Lor and Eric continued to work separately. While Lor and Eric did not seem to want to work together during that math lesson, Eric was the first to congratulate Lor with a "high five" in gym class a few hours later when Lor performed an excellent tumbling routine.

When I asked Mrs. Cavanaugh about the relationship between Lor and Eric, she agreed that sometimes Lor did not want to accept help from Eric. He was sometimes more willing to accept help from another boy in the class, Scott. Scott was perhaps the highest achieving student in the class; when he worked with other students, it was in a way that was very friendly and patient and not at all patronizing or threatening. And if Lor seemed withdrawn or unhappy at times, he was eager to participate at other times. Mrs. Cavanaugh described how Lor had brought some food to share with the class from the Chinese restaurant at which his brother worked. The class enjoyed the food; and Lor brought even more the next day. When he brought food on a third consecutive day, Mrs. Cavanaugh told him that this was very nice, but that they could not have those treats every day. As Mrs. Cavanaugh recalled this story with amusement, her point was that Lor enjoyed participating in classroom activities, and even leading them.

But it seems clear to me that Lor was uncomfortable in the role of the one who needed help. It also seems clear that the reward structure of Cavanaugh's class was such that a number of students would be put in that role. Lor was not the only one who was uncomfortable with this role. During my spring visit, students were preparing outlines for research papers. Mrs. Cavanaugh told them that they could work alone or with a partner if they felt that they needed help. She asked students to raise their hands if they wanted help or wanted to help someone. Three boys, Quinn, Gary, and Ed (who was mentioned in Chapter 4), raised their hands. Quinn said, "I'll help Gary or Ed." Gary immediately spoke up to say, "I don't want help. I want to help someone else. I'll help Ed." Ed accepted the help and, in fact, showed a great eagerness throughout the year to have others help him. Ed received more nominations than any other student in Cavanaugh's class as a desired workmate in the spring. Whereas in most of the 10 classrooms, the most nominations for desired workmates went to students who were simultaneously high achievers, friendly, and cooperative, in Cavanaugh's class the most nominations went to a student who was not a high achiever but who happily accepted the role of one who needed help. This role of one who needed help was one that Ed liked, but students like Lor and Gary were less comfortable with it.

To return to a more direct comparison of Tong in Farr's class and Lor in Cavanaugh's class, I will point out that Tong and most of the other Hmong and low-SES White students at Fawndale Elementary School had attended that school prior to the desegregation plan; it was many of the high-SES students who were new to Fawndale. In contrast, Lor and many of the other Hmong and low-SES White students at Campus Edge were new to the school in the wake of the desegregation plan; most of the high-SES students had attended the school prior to the busing plan. This difference between the two schools probably made it more likely that a classroom structure featuring the roles of "those who gave help" and "those who needed help" would arise in Cavanaugh's class at Campus Edge than in Farr's class at Fawndale.

Jim and Matt

The third pair of students to be compared are Jim and Matt. Jim was introduced in Chapter 4's description of Mrs. Nicholson's classroom. Both Jim and Matt were White boys from low-SES families. Jim was enrolled in Mrs. Nicholson's class at New Forest Elementary School, and Matt was enrolled in Mrs. Fredenburg's class at Fawndale Elementary School.

The point I want to make about Jim and Matt is concise and simple: Each boy was very much at the periphery of his classroom's social structure throughout the school year, but Jim had a more nurturing and personalistic relationship with his teacher than did Matt. In my judgment, this difference allowed Jim to be seen by his classmates in a positive light and as one of whom the teacher approved more often than Matt was. So while neither boy became tightly knit into his classroom's social fabric, I believe Jim ended the school year seeing his fourth-grade experience, and being seen by his classmates, in a somewhat more positive light than Matt did.

To confirm that each boy was very much at the periphery of his classroom's social structure, I will consider the workmate and playmate nominations that each boy received or extended. Jim received no nominations in fall or spring as either a desired workmate or a frequent playmate. In the subgroups identified by KliqueFinder, Jim was identified as a member of a workmate subgroup in cell h in the fall and was removed from the analyses as an isolate in each of the other cases (fall playmate subgroups, spring workmate subgroups, and spring playmate subgroups). He was identified as a member of his fall workmate subgroup only because he extended nominations to two of its other members; he received none. He was not identified as a member of any fall playmate subgroup because he nominated no one as a usual playmate and received no nominations. He was not identified as a member of any spring workmate subgroup or playmate subgroup because nominations from him were missing and he received no nominations.

Matt was identified as a member of a fall workmate subgroup in cell *h*, but—as with Jim—this was only because he extended nominations to two of the other subgroup members; he did not receive any nominations from other subgroup members. He was identified as a member of a spring workmate subgroup in cell *e*, but again, this was only because of nominations he extended to others; he did not receive any from other members. He did receive one fall playmate nomination and was identified as a member of a subgroup in cell *g*. And he received one spring playmate nomination and was identified as a member of a subgroup in cell *a*. But, despite a couple of playmate nominations, Matt—like Jim—was not tightly integrated into his classroom's social structure.

Regarding participation in Fredenburg's classroom, the main times I wrote about Matt in my observational diary were to note that he was not engaged or, in fact, was on the wrong page as the class discussed an assignment. He was not angry or disruptive as some of Fredenburg's students were. He would work with other students when asked to do so. But, in general, he was very withdrawn from classroom activities.

Mrs. Fredenburg did not seem to develop a close relationship with him. The main thing she told me about Matt was that his mother had sent a note one morning asking the teacher not to scold him for not having finished a social studies project about the city of Appleton, Wisconsin. On that day, Mrs. Fredenburg did refrain from scolding Matt. She simply sent him to the school library with a blank sheet of paper to see what he could learn about Appleton while the rest of the students remained in the classroom and worked with the materials they had already collected about the Wisconsin cities that were assigned to them.

The main statement I can make about Matt's presence in the classroom is that he went largely unnoticed. Mrs. Fredenburg paid little attention to him, and other students paid little attention to him. He did not receive the attention that an eager participant would receive. Nor did he receive the attention that a highly disruptive student would receive.

On many days, the same sort of description that applied to Matt would apply to Jim in Nicholson's class. He was not an angry or disruptive student. Rather, he was often simply not engaged with the activities happening around him. He usually worked with other students when asked to do so. But during whole-class lessons or discussions, he would often daydream and not participate.

However, as was mentioned in Chapter 4, Jim had become somewhat more attentive in class by the winter when Mrs. Nicholson had seated him at a more central position in the classroom and when she made greater efforts to call upon him and maintain his attention. Also, the dice game that Jim was asked to teach the class (as recounted in Chapter 4) may have been a one-time occurrence, but it was an important opportunity for Jim to be central to the class's activities and to have his classmates see him in a positive light, receiving praise and support from the teacher.

Furthermore, Mrs. Nicholson used small-group instruction considerably more than any of the other nine teachers. According to my fieldnotes, fully 28% of in-class time in Nicholson's classroom involved small-group activities. The next highest percentage was in Nash's class where 11% of in-class time involved small-group work. Each of the other eight classes spent between 3% and 8% of its time in small groups.

Small-group activities lend themselves to a more personalistic learning environment than do most other task structures (Bossert, 1979; Metz, 1986/1992). In small-group activities, discussions can proceed in a very relaxed tone, with little formality about raising one's hand and following rigid rules. Discipline can be very subtle and not especially public as the teacher may regain a daydreaming student's attention with an arm around the shoulder or may quiet a disruptive student with subtle eye contact. Such subtle disciplinary techniques often are not possible in other learning environments, such as whole-class instruction.

Jim seemed to respond quite well to small-group instruction in Nicholson's class. During my spring visit, I noted that Jim chose to sit next to Mrs. Nicholson as she sat with about half of the class to read and discuss a book called *Immigrant Kids*. All of the students in the small group were highly engaged in the discussion. Jim made a couple of comments and was attentive throughout the activity.

In the descriptions of Kim and Amy above, I drew heavily upon each student's position within her classroom's structure of social relations in explaining their different patterns of participation. Here, in discussing Jim and Matt, I am not drawing upon their positions within the classroom's social structure to explain their different patterns of behavior. They were both very peripheral to the social structure throughout the school year. Nothing about the task and reward structures of the classrooms—or anything else about the classrooms—changed that fact. But the task and reward structures of the two classrooms did differ.

Mrs. Nicholson offered a more personalistic environment and created a few opportunities for Jim to be seen in a positive light by his classmates.

Mrs. Fredenburg's classroom was much less personalistic, and Matt was seldom, if ever, seen by his classmates as being central to classroom activities. While neither boy became highly involved in classroom activities, and neither boy was a highly visible member of his class, Jim would seem to have had a more positive fourth-grade experience than Matt. And while probably neither boy would have been central in his classmates' thoughts and memories of their fourth-grade year, I believe Jim's presence in his class made a slightly stronger and better impression on his classmates than Matt's presence made on his.

DISCUSSION AND CONCLUSIONS

In this chapter, every time I have referred to an individual taking behavioral or attitudinal cues from others or assessing himself or herself relative to others, I have implied the existence of reference-group processes. As Merton and others have developed the theory of reference groups, it is posited that individuals use the norms and activities of groups as frames of reference as they compare and assess themselves and others. As students make assessments about how they fit into the life of the classroom, and how involved they will be in formal and informal activities, they are consciously or subconsciously drawing information from reference groups.

In the past, one criticism of reference-group theory has been that it has offered little or no insight into the process by which individuals select particular reference groups (Deutsch & Krauss, 1965). Throughout this book, I have been building toward a claim that the task and reward structure of a classroom, a teacher's leadership style, and the circumstances that brought a set of students together as classmates influence the structure of peer relations. I have measured and presented some particular structural features of peer relations for each of the LaCrosse classrooms. The emerging structure of peer relations—characterized by specific levels of hierarchy, closure and in-degree for each classroom—helps to define the set of others to whom an individual looks for behavioral and attitudinal cues and for a frame of reference for self-assessment. That is, the structure of peer relations largely defines the reference group to which any particular student looks.

The evidence of Chapter 6 suggested that classrooms such as Mayes's and McCartney's—which combined narrow ranges of tasks and performance settings, high and uniform academic and behavioral standards, and very public environments of discipline and performance—led many students to become situated within quite hierarchical and closed subgroups. In contrast, classrooms featuring more personalism and a wider range of performance settings tended to engender a greater degree of egalitarianism. The extent to which subgroups were partitioned from one another (via high closure and low in-degree) in classrooms featuring high personalism and a wide range of performance settings varied considerably.

As peer relations evolved in one direction or another for each classroom, reference groups became more clearly defined for individual students. Where relatively egalitarian and open peer relations existed, many students related to all of their classmates as an integrated whole rather than to stratified subsets within that whole. Kim in Nash's class was such a student. And in a setting such as Nash's classroom, a desirable situation is likely to be created in which, when asked to do so, students will relate readily, happily, and as equals with most of their classmates, including those who are not their usual workmates and playmates.

Where hierarchical and closed peer relations predominated, many students identified with a more narrow set of students in a context of stratification. Amy in McCartney's class was such a student. The portrayal of Amy and her relations with classmates and teachers also highlighted another important point. In classrooms in which praise and sanction are publicly displayed within the context of a narrow range of performance settings, it is likely that some students will become discouraged and withdrawn while others (like Amy) will participate frequently and eagerly. If something occurs to alter the distribution of the praise and attention, students' levels of enthusiasm and participation in classroom activities can be expected to change as well.

The portrayals of Kim and Amy were intended to illustrate a multistep process in which leadership and task and reward structures affect peer relations, which, in turn, affect student participation. The portrayals of Lor and Tong were intended to illustrate the fact that students' individual personalities interact with the effects of teacher leadership, tasks, and rewards.

Lor in Cavanaugh's class appeared to be uncomfortable with the role into which he was often placed, that of the student who needed help. Lor's classmate Ed, on the other hand, thrived on this role and became a popular student within a classroom reward structure that guaranteed that some students would be placed in this role. Although it is speculation on my part, I conclude from the comparison of Lor and Tong that Lor would have preferred to have found himself in Farr's classroom, sitting alongside Tong. If Lor had found himself there, I am willing to speculate that his interactions with classmates would not have been very different from Tong's patterns of interaction.

Finally, the portrayals of Jim and Matt highlighted a couple of boys who remained peripheral to their classrooms' social structures. Some combination of their social, emotional, and academic development kept them from holding places of centrality and influence in their classes. One might be able to imagine a classroom environment that would have significantly changed these boys' social standing, but certainly neither Nicholson's classroom environment nor Fredenburg's classroom environment accomplished this. Nonetheless, the personalism and time dedicated to small-group activities in Nicholson's classroom offered some positive experiences to Jim that were seemingly absent for Matt in Fredenburg's classroom.

9

Implications for
Educational Research
and Practice

Schools in the United States are serving increasingly heterogeneous student populations. With high levels of migration from other countries and mobility within our borders, schools in the coming decades can expect to encounter more and more racial and ethnic diversity among their students. These trends will be augmented if school districts pursue explicit policies to minimize between-school differences by socioeconomic status (as the LaCrosse district did) or by race and ethnicity (but these efforts seem to be decreasing, as Orfield and Eaton (1996) report with concern).

I do not mean to discourage efforts like the LaCrosse one. To the contrary, I applaud that district's intentions. But with increasing diversity, it seems clear that increased attention must be given to the ways students mix and relate as classmates and to the effects of various aspects of classroom organization and teacher leadership upon students' social relations.

This chapter summarizes the main findings and lessons from the previous chapters. In addition to being directed to the research community, it is intended to be useful to school administrators and teachers who want to encourage participation and feelings of attachment among all students in heterogeneous classrooms. I hope my conclusions will be useful where desegregation efforts are being made and, more generally, wherever diverse sets of students are being brought together as classmates.

This chapter acknowledges some of the issues raised by this study that demand further attention. There is great need for continuing research on issues of classroom organization, culture, and student participation. I hope that current work in these areas will continue, and that new investigations will be initiated.

155

REVISITING FIVE CONDITIONS FOR IMPROVED
INTERGROUP RELATIONS

What are the most concrete things this study has revealed about how to facilitate integration? What has this study shown about the ways in which adults' educational philosophies, decisions, and actions affect students' patterns of peer relations and participation? To answer these questions I want to return to Chapter 2's qualifications to the contact hypothesis that specify conditions necessary for equal-status contact among students. According to those qualifications, which are the cumulative product of others' theory and research, students' selections of favored peers, rates of classroom participation, and amounts and types of interaction with teachers can only become unrelated to the students' memberships in groups defined by things like socioeconomic status or race when the following conditions are met (Cook, 1978; Miller & Brewer, 1984):

1. Students' contact with one another occurs in circumstances that define the status of students from different social groups as equal.
2. The attributes of students from a disliked or stereotyped group disconfirm the prevailing stereotyped beliefs about them.
3. The setting in which students interact encourages, or perhaps requires, a mutually interdependent relationship, that is, cooperation in the achievement of a joint goal.
4. The setting in which students interact has high acquaintance potential; that is, it promotes association of the sort that reveals enough detail about the members of different groups to encourage seeing individuals as individuals rather than as people with stereotyped group characteristics.
5. The social norms of the setting in which students interact favor group equality and egalitarian intergroup association.

Nothing in this study of the LaCrosse classrooms refutes the idea that these five conditions must be fulfilled in order for integration and equal-status contact to emerge when groups of students are brought together in new combinations. A lot of trends in the LaCrosse data add credence to the claim that these conditions must be met to facilitate integration. By reviewing specific classrooms among the 10 that came closest to fulfilling or failing to fulfill each of the conditions, I can highlight concrete examples of practices that educators might want to emulate or avoid as they pursue egalitarian peer relations and participation among their students.

Equal Status Circumstances and Norms of Equality

I can show the importance of the first and fifth conditions above by reviewing a few facts about Mrs. Farr's and Mrs. Cavanaugh's classrooms. These were the two classrooms featured in Chapter 8's portrayals of Tong and Lor. While both of these teachers employed definite strategies to draw all students into the activities of their classrooms, it seems that Farr's class came much closer to having students' contact with one another occur in circumstances that defined the status of all students—whether low- or high-SES, Hmong or White—as equal. It also seems that Farr's class came closer to having social norms that favored group equality and egalitarian inter-group association.

Cavanaugh's class did feature warm and supportive peer relations, and workmate and playmate nominations did cross lines of race and SES. But the qualitative accounts given in Chapters 4 and 8 should make clear that the circumstances under which students were interacting and the norms of the classroom did not really favor equality among different students' roles. The accounts of Ed, Bruce, Lor, and Gary being placed in the roles of those who needed help illustrated how Mrs. Cavanaugh worked to spark participation from all students, but at the expense of norms of equality and egalitarianism.

In contrast, the high and uniform standards of Farr's classroom, coupled with a wide range of performance settings, encouraged egalitarian norms by communicating to students that the paths to status and praise were the same for all. These paths featured variety, with the implication that most students would find that they could excel in traveling at least some of them. And while different students might excel on different paths, the same set of paths and the same social roles were being offered to all students.

I am claiming that Farr's class came closer than Mrs. Cavanaugh's to defining the status of all students as equal and to having norms of equality and egalitarianism because of aspects of teacher's leadership, tasks, and rewards. Further, I am claiming that the effects of the differences between Farr's and Cavanaugh's classes could be seen in students' choices of workmates and playmates and in their patterns of participation in the classroom.

Consider that peer choices in Farr's class were characterized by a trend toward greater egalitarianism as the school year proceeded. This trend could be seen in the fall-to-spring change in distributions of workmate nominations in the class as a whole (Table 5.1 and Figure 5.11). It could also be seen in the changing distributions of workmate and playmate nominations within cohesive subgroups (Figures 6.5 and 6.6). Cavanaugh's class, in contrast, was characterized by a trend toward greater hierarchy as the school year proceeded. Again, this trend was seen whether we looked at workmate nominations in the class as a whole or workmate and playmate nominations within subgroups.

Of course, the relatively hierarchical relations in Cavanaugh's class did not mean that Hmong and low-SES students were consistently the least popular and least engaged students in the class. On the contrary, earlier chapters illustrated the centrality of the low-SES White boy named Ed in Cavanaugh's class: Ed was the student who most readily embraced the role of the one who needed help; and, in a class in which status and praise could be won by reaching out to those who needed help, Ed became a very popular workmate. But this complex situation actually illustrates the point that classrooms in which tasks and rewards work against defining students from different social groups as equal and against norms of equality will not engender egalitarian peer relations. Even if a low-SES student like Ed becomes very central in such a classroom, he probably does so precisely because he occupies a role that is distinct from the roles of many others.

The data of this study do not allow me to evaluate the long-term social or cognitive benefits or harms of being a student in classrooms like Farr's as opposed to classrooms like Cavanaugh's. But if creating classrooms in which students' roles are less differentiated from one another is an educational end in itself, my study leads to a recommendation to emulate many aspects of Farr's class. To do so implies (1) communicating to all students that they will be held accountable to high and uniform academic and disciplinary standards, (2) featuring a fairly wide range of featured and rewarded topics and learning settings, and (3) avoiding an entrenched contrast between those who need help and those who give help.

Providing High Acquaintance Potential and Disconfirming Stereotypes

The importance of the second and fourth conditions for integration and equal-status contact can be illustrated by reviewing a few features of Mr. Rettinger's and Mr. Mayes's classes. I contend that Rettinger's classroom had high acquaintance potential. This high acquaintance potential was achieved because of the classroom's very wide range of topics and settings. Classroom activities and interactions revealed enough detail about students' personalities, interests, and abilities to encourage students to see one another as individuals rather than as people with stereotyped group characteristics. And with such detail revealed, students' attributes often, but not always, disconfirmed stereotypes or preconceptions.

Rettinger's classroom, more than any other in the study, was characterized by a wide range of topics and settings. Classroom activities included some very public displays of academic performance. At times, as in the case of the game of Around the World described in Chapter 4, the public displays and comparisons appeared to be risky because of the potential for great mismatches between students. But that very game of Around the World was a case of an unexpected winner—a student who was not generally regarded as an academic or social leader—emerging victorious and receiving congratulations from his teacher and classmates. I contend that the wide array of performance opportunities in Rettinger's class increased the likelihood of stereotypes and preconceived notions being disconfirmed. And a disconfirming of stereotypes should lead to greater egalitarianism.

In fact, as was true for Farr's class, peer choices in Rettinger's class were characterized by greater egalitarianism as the year proceeded. Fall-to-spring changes in this direction were seen for workmate nominations in the class as a whole and for workmate and playmate nominations within subgroups.

But it is important to recognize that a wide range of performance settings does not have unlimited power to disconfirm stereotypes and, thus, to spark equal-status contact and integration. If educators embrace the strategy of offering students many and varied opportunities to see and learn about one another, they must accept the fact that sometimes stereotypes or preconceptions will be shown to be accurate. The special education students in Rettinger's class were not embraced by other students as workmates or playmates either early or late in the school year. Mainstream students' preconceptions of their special education classmates seemed to be that these other students did not have the patience, cooperative skills, academic skills, or general patterns of behavior that were desired in workmates and playmates. Ongoing interaction only seemed to deepen these beliefs.

These facts about special education students do not lead me away from recommending Mr. Rettinger's organization of tasks and rewards, however. Mr. Rettinger was successful in getting his students to see beyond stereotypes. And his success in this area did seem to contribute to increased egalitarianism in peer relations. But a recommendation to match Mr. Rettinger's wide array of tasks and rewards must be coupled with an acknowledgment of the limits of this strategy for disconfirming stereotypes. To improve relations between mainstream and special education students would have required additional strategies, efforts, and, perhaps, staffing. Such additions, however, would most likely supplement rather than replace the strategies Mr. Rettinger employed.

In contrast to Rettinger's classroom, I contend that Mayes's classroom had high visibility but low acquaintance potential. That is, his classroom afforded students ample opportunity to see one another but only to see one another's traits, behaviors, and abilities within a narrow range of settings. This coupling of frequent but narrow viewing seemed to discourage students from moving beyond stereotypes in order to see others as individuals. Further, it was largely irrelevant whether individuals' attributes did not conform to prevailing stereotypes because many attributes were never given the chance to be seen.

Mayes's classroom seems to illustrate what is likely to happen when high and uniform standards for academic performance and behavior are paired with a narrow range of featured and rewarded topics and settings. As the analyses of workmate and playmate nominations showed, peer relations in such a classroom are likely to become increasingly hierarchical and increasingly fractionalized, with distinct and closed cliques.

While I stand by the claim that Rettinger's class was characterized by a high level of personalism and a wide range of performance settings, and that these created an environment of high acquaintance potential, some difficult issues remain. Although peer relations in Rettinger's class moved toward greater egalitarianism during the year, and although there was some movement toward lower closure and higher in-degree (both signs of less distinct boundaries between cliques) among workmate subgroups, flows of student preferences did not come to be independent of race and SES. Specifically, at both the beginning and end of the school year, Asian American students in Rettinger's class were highly likely to nominate one another, and they were relatively unlikely to receive nominations from non-Asian students. As Chapter 7 reported, similar patterns were found for Nicholson's class and Clark's class.

It is important to stress that relations between Hmong students and White students in these classes were not hostile or characterized by apparent dislike. Indeed, if the teachers asked White and Hmong students to work together, the students did so quite happily. But in these classrooms, which seemed to be characterized by high acquaintance potential and to encourage equal-status contact, students' expressed preferences remained linked to the groupings defined by race and SES.

A couple of possible explanations exist, and they both merit further study. First, I acknowledged in Chapter 4 that I have wondered in retrospect whether I was not sufficiently attuned to subtleties by which some students were drawn into classroom activities via personalism and appeals to cultural capital more than other students were. That is, I stated in Chapter 4 that if a teacher attempts to draw personal experiences and student backgrounds into the classroom for learning purposes, it matters whether all members of the classroom are encouraged, empowered, and inclined to share and contribute or whether the experiences and cultural backgrounds of some are featured and celebrated to the exclusion of others.

If it is true that, in classrooms such as Rettinger's, Nicholson's, and Clark's, appeals to personalism did not reach all students equally, this might explain the continuing segregation in workmate and playmate preferences by race. If, for example, Hmong students did not feel empowered or inclined to share their personal experiences or did not feel that their experiences were relevant to classroom proceedings, other students may have had very limited opportunities to learn about the individual skills, interests, and personalities of particular Hmong classmates. It would follow logically that new friendships, based on common interests or dispositions and overriding social divisions based on race, would be unlikely to form.

Another possibility is that some of the broader social and cultural contexts of students' families had influences that I was not able to study. Chapter 1 referred to research that has shown that Hmong parents and grandparents perceive difficult tensions between encouraging their children to thrive in the American educational system and worrying that traditional Hmong values, language, and culture will be weakened (Chan, 1994; Hones, 1999a; Miyares, 1998). Hmong children may be receiving some forms of discouragement, or at least a lack of encouragement, to form close bonds of friendship with non-Hmong classmates. Some evidence along these lines has been reported previously (Hones, 1999a). Similarly, it may be that non-Hmong children perceived from their homes or neighborhoods discouragement or a lack of encouragement about forming close friendships with their Hmong classmates. In my study, I was not able to collect first-hand information on these issues of family, neighborhood, and cultural priorities and beliefs that may vary by race and ethnicity. However, a body of research exists in these areas, and continuing pursuits in these directions will be very valuable.

Encouragement of Cooperation

A comparison of Mrs. Nicholson's and Mrs. McCartney's classrooms illustrates the importance of the third condition for integration and equal-status contact. Mrs. Nicholson put much more emphasis on small-group work and student interactions that explicitly required cooperation than did Mrs. McCartney. According to my fieldnotes, fully 28% of in-class time in Nicholson's classroom involved small-group activities. In contrast, only 3% of in-class time in McCartney's classroom was spent in small groups.

As Chapter 8 recounted, when Mrs. McCartney did ask students to work in small groups, many students were disinclined to do so. The ability to function productively in small groups is a skill that is learned largely through experience. I think the limited emphasis on small-group work in McCartney's class contributed to the unwillingness or inability of students to work effectively in such groups on the rare occasions when they were asked to do so. Further, I think the paucity of small-group interaction contributed to the trends toward distinct and closed cliques of workmates and playmates in the class. In teacher-led activities students were not regularly encouraged or required to develop close relationships with revolving sets of classmates in small groups. In association with this fact, students' voluntary choices of workmates and playmates were not wide-ranging or inclusive.

Not all of the small-group activities in Nicholson's class involved the carefully planned combinations of individual and collective incentives and accountability that characterize the models of cooperative learning developed by Cohen (1994), Johnson and Johnson (1994), Slavin (1995), and others. Nonetheless, Mrs. Nicholson's considerable emphasis on small-group work did lead her students to interact very directly with one another in many combinations and to depend upon one another for successful completion of tasks. Her students displayed noticeable communication and cooperation skills when working in small groups. Mrs. Nicholson had these skills of her students available to her so that she could accomplish other goals, such as creating an opportunity to feature and celebrate the contributions of the low-SES student named Jim and his dice game of Five Thousand, as recounted in Chapter 8. I am quite sure that Mrs. Nicholson's emphasis on small-group work and cooperation contributed to the trends away from closure and hierarchy as her class proceeded through the school year.

A considerable body of prior research has shown how classroom environments stressing cooperation ease tensions among students and strengthen positive relations (Cohen & Lotan, 1997; Metz, 1986/1992; Schofield, 1982/ 1989; Slavin, 1980). In contrast, the many competitive aspects pervasive in schooling have been shown to reinforce tensions and negative sentiments among students in many cases. While the evidence from the LaCrosse classrooms largely supports these prior theories and findings, in Chapter 4 (and in the preceding section of this chapter) I gave considerable attention to the anecdote about Mr. Rettinger's very public game of Around the World in order to offer an observation about a seemingly positive function of certain competitions. In that anecdote, a highly visible and competitive mathematics activity took place within the context of a classroom that featured and rewarded a very wide range of tasks and competencies. When that combination is present, competitive activities may serve to challenge students' perceptions of academic and social rankings among their classmates.

This observation is certainly not meant to downplay the importance of encouraging cooperation in pursuit of student learning and positive peer relations, but it does suggest that further studies of the interplay of competition, visibility, and the breadth of a classroom's featured tasks and activities might be worthwhile.

FINAL THOUGHTS

James Coleman (1994) articulated a vision of sociology as a discipline that should have social systems (in some cases, small ones; in other cases, large ones) rather than individuals as its primary units of analysis. He noted the strengths and insights of the community studies in American sociology during the first half of the 1900s. These studies were directed toward characterizing communities and toward discovering norms and values, status systems, social cleavages, and the ways in which all these affected peoples' lives and the community's functioning.

I think this vision is a wise and powerful one not just for those who want to advance sociology as a discipline, but also for those who want to use sociological analysis to improve schools. As school systems proceed with their day-to-day teaching of students, and especially when they attempt to implement bold policy initiatives, educators and the researchers who wish to support them should think carefully about implications for the structure and substance of group life. They should consider potential sources of group solidarity and potential cleavages. They should attempt to discern whether norms of equality and cooperation are being engendered or discouraged.

LaCrosse's socioeconomic balance plan certainly rates as a fairly bold initiative. The details of community debate and protest in Chapter 1 confirm that it sparked strong emotions among the affected parties. In studying 10 classrooms over the course of a year in the wake of this balance plan, I have tried to be true to Coleman's vision. I have attempted to describe and explain evolving patterns of social relations as important outcomes of the schooling process. In turn, I have traced the effects of social structure on students' feelings of belonging and comfort with participation.

The study has demonstrated the multistep process by which leadership and task and reward structures affect visibility, observability, and observedness—opportunities to see and be seen, to speak and be heard—and, relatedly, the range of norms, attitudes, and behaviors that are featured in daily classroom life. Within this context, patterns of peer relations emerge and evolve. Students relate to their classmates in more or less hierarchical fashion, and within cohesive subgroups that are more or less closed and divided from one another. These aspects of peer relations—hierarchy and closure—affect the extent to which individuals feel attachment and allegiance to the entire class as an integrated whole or to distinct cliques within the larger class. They affect feelings of belonging and participation.

Among the most important associations demonstrated by the study is the one between wide ranges of featured and rewarded topics and activities and egalitarian structures. The LaCrosse data has also shown evidence of strict and public discipline, high and uniform standards, and a narrow range of topics and activities engendering closed and stratified subgroup structures.

Clearly, how teachers teach and organize their classrooms affects students' preferences of workmates and playmates and the structure of peer networks. In turn, children's locations in peer networks shape their feelings of belonging and participation in classroom life. Outcomes are sometimes sadly ironic and not consistent with teachers' probable goals. A teacher committed to implementing high and uniform standards for performance—seemingly an equality-minded effort—can actually prompt higher levels of within-class stratification among students, especially if the range of tasks and rewards is narrow. A setting that begins by being highly public in nature can evolve to a point at which students' attentions are focused within narrow subgroups rather than extending to the entire class. On the other hand, classroom organization and leadership have wonderful potential to engender cohesion, cooperation, integration, and participation, and that point is an encouraging one to carry forward.

Appendix

Student Sociometric Survey Instrument

[These questions were administered to each class during the fifth week of the school year, and again in April or May. A group interview format was used in which I provided oral instructions and students wrote their answers on the questionnaires. One question that was asked only in the fall, and two that were asked only in the spring, are indicated as such.]

Name: _____

What are some of your favorite things to do at recess?

Who do you usually play with at recess?
[My instructions to the students were that they could name up to five friends, but did not need to name that many if they had just a few friends with whom they usually played.]

A science project you would like to do:
[My instructions were that students should imagine that their teacher came into the classroom one morning and announced that they were going to do a science project. It could be anything they wanted, as long as it was about science and was educational.]

Two classmates you would like to work with:
[My instructions were that students should imagine that the teacher said that the science project was going to be a group project and that they should choose partners. Students should choose people with

whom they would enjoy working and with whom they would do a
good job.]

Favorite things to do after school:
    [fall only]

Friends you usually see after school:
    [fall only]

Clubs and activities you do at school:
    [spring only]

Classmates who have been to your house this year:
    ["This year" was added in spring only.]

References

Allport, G. W. (1954). *The nature of prejudice.* Cambridge, MA: Addison-Wesley.

Barr, R., & Dreeben, R. (1983). *How schools work.* Chicago: University of Chicago Press.

Berry, J. W. (1984). Cultural relations in plural societies: Alternatives to segregation and their sociopsychological implications. In N. Miller & M. B. Brewer (Eds.), *Groups in contact: The psychology of desegregation* (pp. 11–27). Orlando, FL: Academic Press.

Bidwell, C. E. (1965). The school as a formal organization. In J. G. March (Ed.), *Handbook of organizations* (pp. 972–1018). Chicago: Rand-McNally.

Bossert, S. T. (1979). *Tasks and social relationships in classrooms.* Cambridge, U.K.: Cambridge University Press.

Chan, S. (Ed.). (1994). *Hmong means free: Life in Laos and America.* Philadelphia: Temple University Press.

Cohen, E. G. (1984). The desegregated school: Problems in status power and interethnic climate. In N. Miller & M. B. Brewer (Eds.), *Groups in contact: The psychology of desegregation* (pp. 77–96). Orlando, FL: Academic Press.

Cohen, E. G. (1994). *Designing groupwork: Strategies for heterogeneous classrooms* (2nd ed.). New York: Teachers College Press.

Cohen, E. G. (1997). Equity in heterogeneous classrooms: A challenge for teachers and sociologists. In E. G. Cohen & R. A. Lotan (Eds.), *Working for equity in heterogeneous classrooms: Sociological theory in practice* (pp. 3–14). New York: Teachers College Press.

Cohen, E. G., & Lotan, R. A. (1995). Producing equal-status interaction in the heterogeneous classroom. *American Educational Research Journal, 32,* 99–120.

Cohen, E. G., & Lotan, R. A. (Eds.). (1997). *Working for equity in heterogeneous classrooms: Sociological theory in practice.* New York: Teachers College Press.

Coleman, J. S. (1994). A vision for sociology. *Society, 32,* 29–34.

Coleman, J. S., Kelly, S. D., & Moore, J. A. (1975). *Trends in school segregation, 1968–73.* Washington, DC: Urban Institute.

Cone, C. A., & Perez, B. E. (1986). Peer groups and organization of classroom space. *Human Organization, 45,* 80–88.

Cook, S. W. (1978). Interpersonal and attitudinal outcomes in cooperating interracial groups. *Journal of Research and Development in Education, 12,* 97–113.

Cook, S. W. (1984). Cooperative interaction in multiethnic contexts. In N. Miller & M. B. Brewer (Eds.), *Groups in contact: The psychology of desegregation* (pp. 155–185). Orlando, FL: Academic Press.

Deutsch, M., & Krauss, R. M. (1965). *Theories in social psychology.* New York: Basic Books.

Dreeben, R. (1968). *On what is learned in school.* Reading, MA: Addison-Wesley.

Frank, K. A. (1993). *Identifying cohesive subgroups.* Unpublished doctoral dissertation, University of Chicago.

Frank, K. A. (1995). Identifying cohesive subgroups. *Social Networks, 17,* 27–56.

Frank, K. A. (1996). Mapping interactions within and between cohesive subgroups. *Social Networks, 18,* 93–119.

Gerard, H. B., & Miller, N. (1975). *School desegregation.* New York: Plenum.

Hallinan, M. T. (1979). Structural effects on children's friendships and cliques. *Social Psychological Quarterly, 42,* 43–54.

Hallinan, M. T. (1980). Patterns of cliquing among youth. In H. C. Foot, A. J. Chapman, & J. R. Smith (Eds.), *Friendship and social relations in children* (pp. 321–342). Chichester, U.K.: John Wiley.

Hallinan, M. T., & Tuma, N. B. (1978). Classroom effects on change in children's friendships. *Sociology of Education, 51,* 270–282.

Hendricks, G. L., Downing, B. T., & Deinard, A. S. (Eds.). (1986). *The Hmong in transition.* New York: Center for Migration Studies.

Hochschild, J. L. (1984). *The new American dilemma: Liberal democracy and school desegregation.* New Haven, CT: Yale University Press.

Homans, G. C. (1992). *The human group.* New Brunswick, NJ: Transaction. (Original work published 1950)

Hones, D. F. (1999a). Crises, continuity, and the refugee: Educational narratives of a Hmong father and his children. *Journal of Contemporary Ethnography, 28,* 166–198.

Hones, D. F. (1999b). Making peace: A narrative of a bilingual liaison, a school and a community. *Teachers College Record, 101,* 106–134.

Hopkins, T. K. (1964). *The exercise of influence in small groups.* Totowa, NJ: Bedminster Press.

Hutchison, R., & McNall, M. (1994). Early marriage in a Hmong cohort. *Journal of Marriage and the Family, 56,* 579–590.

Johnson, D. W., & Johnson, R. T. (1994). *Learning together and alone: Cooperative, competitive, and individualistic learning* (4th ed.). Englewood Cliffs, NJ: Prentice-Hall.

LaCrosse City Directory. (1993). Kansas City, MO: R. L. Polk.

LaCrosse Tribune. (1992a). Boundary concern put to rest. August 6, p. B3.

LaCrosse Tribune. (1992b). Effect of school transfers still unknown. August 16, p. B3.

LaCrosse Tribune. (1992c). New busing begins. August 23, p. B2.

LaCrosse Tribune. (1992d). Riding the "roller-coaster." July 12, p. B2.

LaCrosse Tribune. (1992e). Rush to transfer. August 23, p. B2.

LaCrosse Tribune. (1992f). Time is nigh for school busing. August 23, p. B1.

LaCrosse Tribune. (1993a). Back to the polls. April 4, p. B1.

LaCrosse Tribune. (1993b). Candidates' differences clear. April 2, p. A9.

LaCrosse Tribune. (1993c). Controversy a draw in city. April 6, p. A1.

LaCrosse Tribune. (1993d). Courts foil attempts to thwart the voters' will. April 9, p. A4.

LaCrosse Tribune. (1993e). Hmong celebrate Vue's history-making victory. April 8, p. B1.

LaCrosse Tribune. (1993f). Hmong odyssey: A special report. October 2, pp. S1–12.

LaCrosse Tribune. (1993g). It's a sweep. April 7, p. A1.

LaCrosse Tribune. (1993h). LaCrosse school board. April 4, p. B2.

LaCrosse Tribune. (1993i). School board epic continues. April 4, p. A1.

LaCrosse Tribune. (1993j). School heat adds to voter turnout. April 7, p. A1.

LaCrosse Tribune. (1993k). Your views: Mayor, council, school board races. April 1, 1993, p. A4.

LaCrosse Tribune. (1994). Wisconsin leads U.S. in Asian child poverty. February 17, p. A1.

Lotan, R. A. (1997). Complex instruction: An overview. In E. G. Cohen & R. A. Lotan (Eds.), *Working for equity in heterogeneous classrooms: Sociological theory in practice* (pp. 15–27). New York: Teachers College Press.

Marsh, C. (1988). *Exploring data: An introduction to data analysis for social scientists.* Cambridge, U.K.: Polity Press.

Marshall, H. H., & Weinstein, R. S. (1984). Classroom factors affecting students' self-evaluations: An interactional model. *Review of Educational Research, 54,* 301–325.

McNall, M., Dunnigan, T., & Mortimer, J. T. (1994). The educational achievement of the St. Paul Hmong. *Anthropology and Education Quarterly, 25,* 44–65.

Merton, R. K. (1968). *Social theory and social structure.* New York: Free Press.

Metz, M. H. (1978). *Classrooms and corridors: The crisis of authority in desegregated secondary schools.* Berkeley: University of California Press.

Metz, M. H. (1992). *Different by design: The context and character of three magnet schools.* New York: Routledge. (Original work published 1986)

Miller, N. (1983). Peer relations in desegregated schools. In J. L. Epstein & N. Karweit (Eds.), *Friends in school: Patterns of selection and influence in secondary schools* (pp. 201–217). New York: Academic Press.

Miller, N., & Brewer, M. B. (1984). The social psychology of desegregation: An introduction. In N. Miller & M. B. Brewer (Eds.), *Groups in contact: The psychology of desegregation* (pp. 1–8). Orlando, FL: Academic Press.

Mills, N. (Ed.). (1979). *Busing U.S.A.* New York: Teachers College Press.

Milwaukee Journal. (1992a). LaCrosse schools to integrate rich and poor. January 26, p. 5.

Milwaukee Journal. (1992b). No last chapter in boundary uproar. August 2, p. 5.

Milwaukee Sentinel. (1993). LaCrosse busing travels bumpy road. March 18, p. 1A.

Miyares, I. M. (1998). *The Hmong refugee experience in the United States: Crossing the river.* New York: Garland.

Olzak, S., Shanahan, S., & West, E. (1994). School desegregation, interracial exposure, and antibusing activity in contemporary urban America. *American Journal of Sociology, 100,* 196–241.

Orfield, G., & Eaton, S. E. (1996). *Dismantling desegregation: The quiet reversal of Brown v. Board of Education.* New York: New Press.

Parsons, T. (1951). *The social system.* New York: Free Press.

Parsons, T. (1959). The school class as a social system: Some of its functions in American society. *Harvard Educational Review, 29,* 297–318.

Pettigrew, T. F. (1969). Racially separate or together. *Journal of Social Issues, 25,* 43–69.

Rist, R. C. (1978). *The invisible children: School integration in American society.* Cambridge, MA: Harvard University Press.

Rist, R. C. (Ed.). (1979). *Desegregated schools: Appraisals of an American experiment.* New York: Academic Press.

Rivkin, S. G. (1994). Residential segregation and school integration. *Sociology of Education, 67,* 279–292.

Rogers, M., Hennigan, K., Bowman, C., & Miller, N. (1984). Intergroup acceptance in classroom and playground settings. In N. Miller & M. B. Brewer (Eds.), *Groups in contact: The psychology of desegregation* (pp. 213–227). Orlando, FL: Academic Press.

Rosenholtz, S. J. (1982). Organizational determinants of classroom social power. *Journal of Experimental Education, 50,* 83–87.

Rosenholtz, S. J. (1985). Treating problems of academic status. In J. Berger & M. Zelditch, Jr. (Eds.), *Status, rewards, and influence* (pp. 445–470). San Francisco: Jossey-Bass.

Rosenholtz, S. J., & Cohen, E. G. (1983). Back to basics and the desegregated school. *The Elementary School Journal, 83,* 515– 527.

Rosenholtz, S. J., & Rosenholtz, S. H. (1981). Classroom organization and the perception of ability. *Sociology of Education, 54,* 132–140.

Rosenholtz, S. J., & Simpson, C. (1984). Classroom organization and student stratification. *The Elementary School Journal, 85,* 21–37.

Rosenholtz, S. J., & Wilson, B. (1980). The effect of classroom structure on shared perceptions of ability. *American Educational Research Journal, 17,* 75–82.

Rumbaut, R. G. (1989). Portraits, patterns, and predictors of the refugee adaptation process: Results and reflections from the HARP panel study. In D. W. Haines (Ed.), *Refugees as immigrants: Cambodians, Laotians, and Vietnamese in America* (pp. 138–182). Totowa, NJ: Rowman & Littlefield.

Schofield, J. W. (1989). *Black and white in school: Trust, tension, or tolerance?* New York: Teachers College Press. (Original work published 1982)

Schofield, J. W. (1991). School desegregation and intergroup relations: A review of the literature. *Review of Research in Education, 17,* 335–409.

Schofield, J. W. (1995). Promoting positive intergroup relations in school settings. In W. D. Hawley & A. W. Jackson (Eds.), *Toward a common destiny: Improving race and ethnic relations in America* (pp. 257–289). San Francisco: Jossey-Bass.

Simpson, C. (1981). Classroom structure and the organization of ability. *Sociology of Education, 54,* 120–132.

Slavin, R. E. (1980). Cooperative learning. *Review of Educational Research, 50,* 315–342.

Slavin, R. E. (1995). *Cooperative learning: Theory, research, and practice* (2nd ed.). Boston: Allyn and Bacon.

Slavin, R. E., & Hansell, S. (1983). Cooperative learning and intergroup relations: Contact theory in the classroom. In J. L. Epstein & N. Karweit (Eds.), *Friends in school: Patterns of selection and influence in secondary schools* (pp. 93–114). New York: Academic Press.

Slavin, R. E., & Oickle, E. (1981). Effects of cooperative learning teams on student achievement and race relations. *Sociology of Education, 54,* 174–180.

Tammivaara, J. S. (1982). The effects of task structure on beliefs about competence and participation in small groups. *Sociology of Education, 55,* 212–222.

Timm, J. T. (1994). Hmong values and American education. *Equity & Excellence in Education, 27,* 36–44.

Trueba, H. T., Cheng, L., & Ima, K. (1993). *Myth or reality: Adaptive strategies of Asian Americans in California.* Washington, DC: Falmer Press.

Trueba, H. T., Jacobs, L., & Kirton, E. (1990). *Cultural conflict and adaptation: The case of Hmong children in American society.* New York: Falmer Press.

U.S. Department of Commerce. Bureau of the Census. (1992). *1990 Census of population and housing summary tape file 3A* [CD ROM]. Washington, D.C.: Data User Services Division.

Waller, W. (1932). *The sociology of teaching.* New York: John Wiley.

Watson, G. (1947). *Action for unity.* New York: Harper.

Williams, R. M., Jr. (1947). *The reduction of intergroup tensions.* New York: Social Science Research Council.

Yamaguchi, K. (1992). Accelerated failure-time regression models with a regression model of surviving fraction: An application to the analysis of 'permanent employment' in Japan. *Journal of the American Statistical Association, 87,* 284–292.

Index

Academic standards, 41, 63
  peer relations and, 68
  in subject classrooms, 64
Acquaintance potential, 38, 45–46
Allport, G. W., 10
Amy (Maple Grove student profile), 141–145, 153
Armor, D., 7
Ascriptive characteristics, intergroup relations and, 80–81, 88, 91, 94–97, 111–135

Balance plan. *See* Desegregation plan
Barr, R., 15
Berry, J. W., 9
Bidwell, C. E., 15, 18
Bossert, S. T., 15–16, 18–20, 39, 53, 57, 151
Bowman, C., 12
Brewer, M. B., 10, 156

Campus Edge Elementary School. *See also* Cavanaugh classroom; Clark classroom
  climate and organizational characteristics, 26–27
  gender composition of subgroups, 97
  Lor (student profile), 146–148, 153
  low-SES students in, 24, 26, 51
  parental involvement, 26–27
  racial and socioeconomic composition of subgroups, 98
Cavanaugh classroom (Campus Edge)
  academic standards, 64
  described, 51–53
  disciplinary standards, 64
  dyadic playmate nominations in spring, 124
  dyadic workmate nominations in spring, 119
  equal-status contact and, 157–158
  Lor (student profile), 146–148, 153

  range of performance settings, 64
  student characteristics, 35–36, 51, 96
  student personalism, 64
  subgroup structure in, 94–96, 100, 102, 105, 106, 107, 108, 119, 124
  teacher personalism, 64
  workmate nominations for fall and spring, 72, 77, 78
Centrality, 14
Chan, S., 3–4, 5, 161
Cheng, L., 4
Clark classroom (Campus Edge)
  academic standards, 64
  described, 49–51
  disciplinary standards, 64
  dyadic playmate nominations in spring, 124
  dyadic workmate nominations in spring, 119
  range of performance settings, 64
  student characteristics, 35–36, 51, 96
  student personalism, 64
  subgroup structure in, 94–96, 100, 102, 105, 106, 107, 108, 119, 124
  teacher personalism, 64
  workmate nominations for fall and spring, 70, 72, 75, 77, 78
Classroom observation, 34–66
  classification following, 63–65
  descriptions of subject classrooms, 41–63
  descriptive framework for, 37–41
  nature of, 31
Cliques. *See* Intergroup relations
Closure
  defined, 81–82
  intergroup relations and, 104–107, 137, 138, 139
Cohen, E. G., 9, 12, 19, 20, 32–33, 39, 43, 49, 54, 162
Coleman, J. S., 10, 163–164
Cone, C. A., 18, 113

173

About the Author

Stephen Plank is an associate research scientist at Johns Hopkins University's Center for Social Organization of Schools. He received his B.A. from Northwestern University and his M.A. and Ph.D. in sociology from the University of Chicago. He has published articles and book chapters on middle school reform, peer influences on adolescents' career expectations, the transition to postsecondary education or work, and school choice. With James Coleman, Barbara Schneider, and others, he coauthored *Redesigning American Education* (Westview Press, 1997). Plank is also an adjunct assistant professor of sociology at Johns Hopkins University.